CLOSE
ANY DEAL
A. DAVID SILVER'S
SIX-STEP FORMULA
FOR SUCCESS

A. DAVID SILVER

PRENTICE HALL
Englewood Cliffs, New Jersey 07632

Dedication
Claude, Caleb and Dayn

Prentice-Hall International (UK) Limited, *London*
Prentice-Hall of Australia Pty. Limited, *Sydney*
Prentice-Hall Canada, Inc., *Toronto*
Prentice-Hall Hispanoamericana, S.A., *Mexico*
Prentice-Hall of India Private Limited, *New Delhi*
Prentice-Hall of Japan, Inc., *Tokyo*
Simon & Schuster Asia Pte. Ltd., *Singapore*
Editora Prentice-Hall do Brasil, Ltda., *Rio de Janeiro*

© 1992 *by*

PRENTICE HALL
Englewood Cliffs, NJ

10 9 8 7 6 5 4 3

Library of Congress Cataloging-in-Publication Data

Silver, A. David (Aaron David), 1941–
    Close any deal : A. David Silver's 6-step formula for success / A.
David Silver.
        p.   cm.
    Includes index.
    ISBN 0-13-138306-X
    1. Selling.   2. Success in business.   I. Title.
HF5438.25.S57   1992
658.8′5—dc20   91-37160
                                                            CIP

ISBN 0-13-138306-X

PRENTICE HALL
Professional Publishing
Englewood Cliffs, NJ 07632
Simon & Schuster. A Paramount Communications Company

Printed in the United States of America

HOW THIS BOOK WILL HELP YOU

Many deals fall through. Many deals that *do* get off the ground won't succeed. This book will show you how to be a successful deal maker. By following the six-step formula for success, you'll discover proven strategies for turning *no* into *yes,* and compelling your buyer or investor to close the deal.

Deal making can mean many things—from buying antique furniture at 35 percent less than its asking price, to staying out of bankruptcy by refinancing millions of dollars of debt, to raising money to finance a project, to selling distressed real estate at a Tiffany's price. Successful deal-makers make things happen by *leveraging*; that is, persuading others to do something for you that they had no intention of doing before you began talking.

Here are some of the deal-making ventures this book explores:

- How to avoid the tollgates that get in your way and keep you from reaching the decision-makers.
- How to gain the cooperation of your prospective buyer by discovering what motivates him or her.
- How to control the conversation with effective use of questions.
- Tips on using publicity and third-party endorsements to promote an aura of authority about your deal.
- Strategic versus financial buyers—knowing the difference can be money in your pocket.
- How ten of the world's greatest entrepreneurial companies earned millions by solving their buyers' problems.
- How to convince the buyer to act quickly without seeming pushy.
- Key words to listen for that indicate the buyer likes your deal.
- How looking vulnerable can actually give you the competitive edge.

Successful deal-makers can assemble an uncanny number of closed deals—companies, screenplays, real estate properties, and so forth—unsuccessful deal-makers continually miss the opportunity. It's not a question of one person being luckier than the other. The difference is that successful deal-makers understand the six-step process of closing deals.

Many people are simply linear thinkers; that is, they assume that the only way from place to place is accomplished by taking one path, and that path must be the shortest, most direct route. Successful deal-makers learn how to think *associationally*; that is, they know that there are often several paths that will get them to their destination. When someone asks me to raise capital to shoot a movie, my first thought is not "Who's the director?" or "What's the size of the budget?" I want to know how many extras will be in the movie and what their ethnic persuasion is. Why? Because my Rolodex doesn't have the names and telephone numbers of many movie investors, but it does have the names of dozens of economic development directors from local communities with the capital to make loans or grants if a large number of minorities are hired as extras for six to eight weeks. By raising up to $600,000 in local development money, the producer can entice a bankable star and thereafter the millions of dollars necessary to shoot the movie. By thinking associationally rather than linearly, you can access the deal-makers that will say *yes* to the financing of your project.

You'll find out how to get to the heart of a deal: to put a "headline" on your premise to say: "this deal can solve this problem for these people." The *Demonstrable Economic Proposition* (the DEP Factor) is the single most important statement that persuades the buyer to write his or her check.

By following the strategies mapped out in this book, you'll discover how to control, as much as possible, *all* contingencies—and how to convince others to choose *your* deal above all others.

CONTENTS

AUTHOR'S OTHER BOOKS INCLUDE:

THE ENTREPRENEURIAL LIFE
WHO'S WHO IN VENTURE CAPITAL, THREE EDITIONS
ENTREPRENEURIAL MEGABUCKS
WHEN THE BOTTOM DROPS
THE MIDDLE MARKET BUSINESS ACQUISITION DIRECTORY
THE MIDDLE MARKET LEVERAGED FINANCING
    DIRECTORY
THE INSIDE RAIDER
THE BANKRUPTCY, WORKOUT AND TURNAROUND
    MARKET
THE TURNAROUND SURVIVAL GUIDE
YOUR FIRST BOOK OF WEALTH

PART ONE

THE CLOSING PROCESS

SIX STEPS TO A SUCCESSFUL CLOSING

In every situation in which two people communicate, one is always "selling" and the other(s) is potentially "buying." "Selling" includes persuading, teaching, motivating, urging, or convincing the other person or persons to trust, accept, believe in, loan, or invest money in, approve or recognize the idea, concept, outline or description of some event that may occur in the future.

There are six critical steps necessary to close a deal. The following steps describe the tools used in deal making and explain how a winner can be selected:

1. Determine your product's *Demonstrable Economic Proposition* (the DEP factor).

2. Gather data about your noncustomer—the target of your sale.

3. Find the gatekeepers who can block your deal and develop a strategy for "shunning their pikes."

4. Leverage others who can lose if your deal doesn't close.

5. Control the closing meeting with questions.

6. Add a dose of third-party endorsement to your deal.

Let's look at each of these steps more closely.

STEP 1: FIND THE DEP FACTOR

If you were to write a headline about your product or service, what would it say? What single statement would compel people to buy what you are selling? The headline must be the precise solution to the problem shared by your intended buyers. The Demonstrable Economic Proposition (the DEP factor) is a *succinctly stated solution or need that the target buyer is looking for, but that may be, and probably is, unstated.*

Many sellers ignore the issue of finding their unique selling proposition and attempt to close the buyer with other premises such as lower price, more features, after-sale support, more locations, or

24-hour service. But these side issues take profit out of a deal. A brilliantly conceived DEP factor enables the seller to maintain a high profit margin.

Still other sellers, particularly those with industrial or technology-based solutions, obfuscate their headlines with a lengthy explanation of a complex factory bottleneck such as: "If you're using six throws on your 4000 hp reciprocal compressor but only pulling 400 bps, then you need a Ramaframas Compressor with more pull for less hp." Apparently, the unique feature of the Ramaframas Compressor is more power for less cost, but the proposed buyer usually cannot make the mental conversion because the features are hidden in an overly detailed description of the problem. Buyers want a message conveyed in easily recognizable patterns.

Federal Express was burning advertising money needlessly between 1972 and 1974 with headlines that touted "We Own Our Own Planes." The target customer did not give a hoot for such a grand and egocentric statement, and Federal Express was bleeding red ink while searching desperately for its DEP factor: a headline that would set it apart from freight-forwarders. Finally, it discovered that what it was selling was a solution to the anxiety of the shipping clerk, whose job rested precariously on the prompt and certain arrival of his or her company's package at its destination the following day. Federal Express discovered its headline on the verge of filing for bankruptcy protection: "Absolutely, Positively, Overnight"—a money-back guarantee of next day delivery by 10:30 A.M. The rest, as they say, is history.

Every deal must have a headline. Every deal must state a demonstrable economic proposition and answer the question, "What opportunity or need does your deal address?" The DEP factor should compel the buyer to close from the moment he or she sees or hears the headline. However, 90 percent of all sellers either overstate or complicate the problem. Many of us know the headline "The Heartbreak of Psoriasis," but few of us know the product that is used to solve it—or conversely describe the nuts and bolts of the solution conveyance system. This is *centripetal* projecting—looking inward at the mechanics of the concept—rather than *centrifugal*—looking at a description of the solution from the buyers' point of view.

STEP 2: COLLECT DATA ON YOUR
TARGET BUYERS

Who are your prospective buyers? Do they have "open to buys" for what you are selling? Can they pay for it? Once you have found them, how do you qualify them inexpensively? There are horror stories of sellers who have spent months and months trying to sell a buyer only to learn at the closing that there was yet another hurdle to jump.

A fast "no" is as good as a long "yes." If you know all of the buyer's objections upfront, then you have qualified him or her in full. You know exactly what aspects of your deal are going to present the most difficulty: price, terms, delivery schedule, involvement of the buyer, labor intensivity of the buyer, timing or other drawbacks. Clarity is critical to closings.

The needs of prospective buyers may change suddenly due to external events. They may have been open to buys yesterday, and you are too late. In a great number of situations, a deal maker arrives at a prospect's door too early and will have to help the proposed buyer see the need for the deal.

If your deal is too ahead of its time or too out front of the buyers' perception of the problem, you will waste a lot of time and money in qualifying. Pioneers get arrows in their backs. The second guy who enters a market frequently does better than the first because the buyers have been prequalified.

A good example of this: the Honda Motor Company's introduction of the Cub Cadet into the United States in the early 1960s. The postwar baby boom had created a population of millions of young adults who could not afford cars yet whose lifestyles beckoned excitement and freedom. They could afford motorbikes or mopeds, but there existed a negative image about motorbike owners having to do with the Hells' Angels and social ostracism that negatively impacted moped sales in the U.S. Honda countered this negative perception with a positive one of its own—"You meet the nicest people on a Honda"—which blazed the way for Honda to close deals with thousands of bicycle dealers who subsequently closed their own deals with millions of Cub Cadet owners.

To collect data on your target buyer requires one or more forms of market research. Direct-response marketing is the principal means of assessing noncustomer needs in the consumer products marketplace. Johnson & Johnson and Kimberly Clark know the names, addresses, and parents' names of every child born in America within one week of their birth by buying lists from photographers of newborns. The *Wall Street Journal* buys lists of new purchasers of BMWs and Mercedes-Benzes and blitzes them with direct mail. Questionnaires mailed to corporate executives allegedly to elicit their thoughts about the needs of the planet is a good tactic for getting them to talk about what they like to read, drive, eat and do on weekends. Telemarketing as well is becoming an ever more popular means of collecting lots of information quickly and inexpensively.

What does *qualify the prospective buyer* actually mean? It means, ask enough questions upfront to find out what he or she likes and does not like about your deal, without turning him or her off by appearing ill-informed or naive. This is frequently done with *either-or* questions.

For example, if I ask you, "What is your favorite food?" you may have difficulty being specific. But if I ask you, "Do you like meat better than fish?" and if you say "Yes," then follow with "Do you like steak better than hamburgers?" I have qualified you for steak sauces, barbecue grills, and a whole host of related products.

Clarity upfront, even if it is a quick "no" is critical to getting a "yes" out of the buyer. If you substitute assumptions for clarity, you could be going down a blind alley burning up money and time.

STEP 3: FIND THE GATEKEEPERS AND GO AROUND THEM

There are tollgates in front of every consumer highway, erected either by commercial or government opportunists who seized opportunities to block deals—that is, charge a fee for access to the buyers—unless the gatekeeper could be persuaded to turn the pike and let the change-maker pass. It is the gatekeeper's *gut values* that are his or her tollgate. These values can block an innovative plan as thoroughly and completely as can the FDA, one of the most powerful gatekeepers in the country, from stopping an innovative drug from penetrating the market. But the deal-maker can gain the *cooperation* of the gatekeeper by understanding his or her gut values and communicating empathetically.

The Deal That Hatched Federal Express Corporation

When Frederick W. Smith was hammering together the initial $96 million necessary to launch Federal Express Corp., his cooperative strategy involved the following collaboration:

1. *Endorsement:* A report by a consulting firm with freight-forwarding experience that blessed Smith's business plan;

2. *Sponsorship:* An agreement by General Dynamics Corp. to provide a fleet of airplanes plus a portion of the capital to buy them, and long-term financing for the balance;

3. *Endorsement:* Industry-experienced managers joined forces with the 29-year old Smith and began lining up early customers (the name "Federal Express" was selected because Smith and his team were convinced that the Federal Reserve would be the company's most important customer; but it never did play an important role, except as an interested, potential customer that other players could look to as a source of endorsement);

4. *Gatekeepers:* The company's investment banker, Rothschild, Inc., tested the money-raising waters for Federal Express and determined that potential investors were uncomfortable with the concept of flying all packages into a single hub in the middle of the night, sorting them, and flying them out to their destinations in the early hours of the morning. Thus, a nationally-known management consulting firm was hired to bless the concept;

5. *Leverage:* Prudential Insurance Co. agreed to provide a layer of long-term debt subject to the rest of the financing, which was mostly venture capital, coming together. Smith took the subject-to

commitment from Prudential back to General Dynamics, whose feet were getting cold waiting for others to follow its lead. The financing arrangements with General Dynamics were improved to the company's advantage;

6. *Financing:* Given strong managers to supplement Smith's inexperience; two management consultant studies that said the concept would fly; a supplier of airplanes willing to take back a promise of getting paid in the future as partial consideration and willing to partially finance the company; a highly-regarded investment banker shaking the trees for start-up equity capital; and an insurance company willing to provide a layer of long-term debt between the equipment financing and the equity; the $96 million deal that launched Federal Express closed in 1972.

The date of the Federal Express deal is significant because when the price of oil quadrupled two years later, the company almost went bankrupt; one of the reasons for its near failure was the absence of a demonstrable economic proposition.

Every deal that is turned down is done so by a gatekeeper. These gatekeepers exist in every market, and I will show you how to get around them. The most rigid gatekeepers are people who sit on decision-making committees and find it *safer* for their careers to say "no" and to block deals. If your idea has career advancement opportunities for them, they will approve it. But if you can't present your deal to them directly to show them its sound personal benefits, the risk of a turn-down is heightened.

You may think you have the loan officer "sold" when he hears your deal and says, "I like it." But if you let the matter drop there, you will probably not close your deal because you haven't learned anything about what the gatekeepers are thinking. You should ask the following questions of the *deal-messenger*:

"Do you have to present this deal to committee? Who is on the committee? When does it meet? Does a deal require 100 percent approval to close? Who is most likely to block it? What can we do to get his or her approval?"

There are a great number of questions you can pose as you read Chapter Six, including how to gain permission to present your deal to the entire committee rather than having the deal-messenger handle it alone.

STEP 4: LEVERAGE OTHERS
TO HELP CLOSE

You can increase your closing ratio if you are willing to give up some of the credit. More to the point: most deals crater when the seller seeks to retain all of the credit.

In the halls of Congress, where there are 100 senatorial and 521 congressional gatekeepers, the President's acolytes know that to get the President's ideas sponsored as bills, they have to give up the credit to certain Senators or Representatives. The trade-off is not credit for cash flow, it is an IOU for presidential endorsement at election time.

The same technique applies in business. Sam Walton conceived an idea for financing the first of several Wal-Mart stores that he opened with government-guaranteed loans. The local politicians took the credit and got to appear in the local newspapers with their feet on silver shovels or laying cornerstones. Standing in front of the microphones, the politicians announced their pleasure in bringing 50 or so jobs to the community. Walton remained in the background, actively "shoveling" credit to those who needed it. He held onto more equity in the process, which became worth $12 billion.

STEP 5: JUST ASK

Closing can be equated with negotiating. And the key to successful negotiating is to control conversations by asking the following questions: "Are you looking for this kind of property at this time? What is your overall budget for this kind of deal? Have you ever done this kind of deal before? What are your constraints in qualifying this line for your open to buy? Do you have decision-making responsibility in this area? What kind of information do you need to take this deal to committee? When does the committee next meet? Will this deal be presented at that committee meeting? Would it be appropriate for me to attend? Do you need to meet some of the other players, or see the site, or do you need other back-up data?"

Someone (who stands to benefit if there is a closing) should attend the deal meeting with you and take thorough notes on the buyer's responses. The notes can be reviewed later and if you fail to follow-up on one or more of the buyer's answers or statements, you can ask for another meeting or make a telephone call to clarify a point.

Another axiom in successful negotiating is that the party with the most time usually wins. You should stay at the deal meeting until the other side has to leave. An early departure by you will not sit well with the buyer.

Bring one or more of your sponsors to the meeting. If you are applying for a loan with a local government guarantee, bring the guarantor to the meeting. Discuss with the guarantor in advance what you expect him or her to say. One of you should ask, "Is this guarantee going to be acceptable to you?" Listen carefully to the response. If it is a "yes," then ask, "Will you need additional collateral? Can we talk about that?"

The type of conference that you want to achieve at the deal meeting is one that is highly orchestrated, yet animated, with lots of questions and give and take. This is the time to demonstrate your competence as orchestra leader.

STEP 6: USE A THIRD-PARTY ENDORSEMENT

In many instances, the deal meeting will not be decisive. A decision will come later when the buyer has a committee meeting to decide whether or not to accept or kill the deal. In the interim period, it is essential that you provide a *myth of authority:* If you're not selling Sears' paints, then you cannot endow your deal with the same 100 years or so of trustworthy service. But you can get the local media—the newspapers that are read and the television shows that are watched by the people on the committee—to give you a mention, at the very least.

When I fly into Columbus or Dubuque for a deal meeting, I sometimes have my secretary call one or two writers and TV journalists in these cities to schedule an interview. The subject of the interview is the benefit to the community if my deal closes. In most instances, the story will run prior to the committee meeting, and my deal will have the third-party endorsement of the press and, thus, the ring of authority. This is critical to providing information to the gatekeepers on the decision-making committee whom you may not be permitted to sell to in person.

There are no guarantees in the deal business. Some awfully bad deals attract funding from sources who should know better but don't want to be left without a representative deal when a certain trend occurs. Some very good deals never attract sponsorship. Other deals obtain funding, sponsorship, endorsement, and a customer base but fail as businesses six months after launch. DeLorean Motor Company is a case in point. It raised over $150 million through a highly regarded investment bank, Oppenheimer & Co. Some of its funding was provided by the Government of Ireland. Dealers signed up in droves to carry the DeLorean car. Yet the company crashed and burned in less than a year, to the regret of all participants. It is better not to attempt a deal that could become a disaster; however, perceiving problems in advance is often difficult.

1

FINDING OUT WHAT YOUR BUYER WANTS—THE DEP FACTOR

STRATEGIC VERSUS FINANCIAL BUYERS

There are two basic groups of potential buyers: *strategic* and *financial*. The strategic buyer wants the deal for its *opportunity*. The financial buyer wants the deal for its *cash flow* or return on investment. Naturally, the strategic buyer will pay more in order to meet his or her requirements.

Strategic Buyers

When Eli Lilly & Co. paid 15 times revenues for Hybritech in 1987, it did so to obtain a presence in genetic engineering. When Pillsbury paid 26 times earnings for Steak 'n Ale in 1980, it did so to add a dinner-house chain to its restaurant division. When Medtronics paid 8 times revenues for Versaflex in 1990, it did so to broaden its product line and reduce its concentration on pacemakers. Something takes possession of the minds of large corporations when they are on the prowl. Rather than call an exorcist to remove the passion to overpay for a niche business, they pay the price because the egos of the managers drive them to it. Their egos compel them to take over small, interesting niche and regional businesses with the intent to make them large, interesting, national, and international businesses.

Financial Buyers

If the strategic buyers don't come knocking at your door, the financial buyers are likely to. Financial buyers are entrepreneurs with a couple of bucks in their pocket and an understanding of how to accomplish leveraged financings—or investors or lenders whose assignment is to make money with their money.

The former borrow on the assets of your company and repay the debt with the company's cash flow. Let me explain how a leveraged buyout works.

Let's assume that you own a $12-million-revenue electric sign manufacturer. The financial statements submitted to you are shown in Figure 1.1. The LBO entrepreneur makes two quick examinations to see if a leveraged buyout is feasible: (1) to determine how much can be borrowed on the target company's balance sheet; and (2) to determine if the company's cash flow can support the debt service. Assume that he or she intends to offer you five times pretax earnings, or $5 million.

Using conventional borrowing ratios, the LBO entrepreneur estimates the amount of debt that can be borrowed on the target company's balance sheet, as presented in Figure 1.2.

Desktop analysis indicates that he or she can borrow a little more than one half the price he or she intends to offer. By multiplying the entire estimated purchase price by 13 percent (prime plus 2.5 percent) and adding approximately $500,000 per annum to that amount, it can be measured against pretax earnings to determine if the debt can be serviced.

$5,000,000 x .13 =	$ 650,000
Plus Term Loan Repayments	500,000
Total Annual Debt Service	**$1,150,000**

The company's pretax earnings are inadequate to service this debt: $1,000,000 cannot cover $1,150,000.

Figure 1.1
OUTDOOR ELECTRIC SIGN VENDOR BALANCE SHEET

Assets			Liabilities and Net Worth	
Current Assets:			Current Liabilities:	
Cash	$	100	Accounts Payable	$1,400
Accounts Receivable		2,000	Accrued Expenses	600
Inventory		1,400		
Total Current Assets		3,500	Total Current Liabilities	2,000
Fixed Assets:			Long-Term Debt	—
Plant (Net)		500	Net Worth:	
Equipment (Net)		400	Common Stock	500
Other Assets		100	Retained Earnings	2,000
			Total Net Worth	2,500
			TOTAL LIABILITIES AND	
TOTAL ASSETS		$4,500	NET WORTH	$4,500

Operating Statement Latest 12 Months

	Latest Fiscal Year
Sales	$12,000
Cost of Goods Sold	8,700
Gross Profit	3,300
Operating Expenses	2,300
Net Operating Income	1,000
Provision for Taxes	350
Net Profits After Taxes	$ 650
Add-Backs:	
Owner's Salary	$ 250
Owner's Perks	100
Total Adjusted EBIT	$ 1,350

Figure 1.2
LEVERAGABILITY OF THE SELLER

Asset	Book or Liquidation Value	x	Loan Ratio	=	Amount of Loan (In Dollars)
Accts. Receivable	$2,000		.80		$1,600
Inventory	800*		.50		400
Plant	500**		.75		375
Equipment	250**		.75		187
Total					$2,562

* Work in process inventory has been netted out. Borrowers will lend only against finished goods and raw material inventory.

**Estimated liquidation value; that is, the amount that the assets would bring at auction.

However, there are add-backs. The owner has been pulling down $250,000 per annum in salary, and he will retire. His perks—country club, two cars, brother-in-law's overcharges for insurance, and two "business trips" to Hawaii and Europe each year—total $100,000 per annum. When these are added back, the adjusted earnings figure, referred to as earnings before interest and taxes (EBIT), is $1,350,000.

There is more. Your target's depreciation has been $65,000 per year. Thus, the company's EBIT plus depreciation ("EBIT–D") is $1,415,000, which is comfortably above debt service.

Next, the lender will ask the LBO entrepreneur to put up at least 10 percent of the amount of its loan so there will be something at risk. He or she will offer to put up less. You might ask for $6.75 million, which is 5× Adjusted EBIT, while the LBO entrepreneur can raise only $5.5 million. You may have to take back a subordinated note for $1.25 million to get your price. The entrepreneur can buy the company for a cash investment of $250,000 if you finance some of the price.

Tradeoffs in Choosing Between a Strategic and a Financial Buyer

A strategic buyer is likely to close down your operations or your plans to begin a local satellite plant in your community and move your corporation to one of its symbiotic facilities. Your employees could lose their jobs.

Strategic buyers *always pay more* for a deal than do financial buyers. In selling your company to a strategic buyer to obtain a higher price for your company, emphasize all the opportunities for growth that exist that you have been unable to take advantage of due to lack of *key people*. This will be extremely gratifying to the corporation manager-buyer.

Mention that "We should be opening new marketing channels" or "We have thought of the following, but just haven't had the time or the key personnel to implement the program."

When a publishing company is taken over by a strategic buyer or an inside raider, for example, the publishing company's cash flow can be multiplied through the following channels:

- Resale of news stories to other publishers.

- Repackaging of stories as videotapes.

- Repackaging of stories as audiocassettes.

- Seminars led by highly-regarded columnists.

- Capturing critical information on electronic media and reselling it as a "news utility" such as Reuters and the Telerate subsidiary of the *Wall Street Journal.*

- Books made up of special-interest articles, such as *The New York Times Cookbook.*

- Articles on topical issues such as health care, diet, exercise, recipes, and gardening sold to small-town newspapers as "Sunday Features."

- Joint ventures with direct mail firms that seek to sell products via mail order to the newspaper's readers.

- Ownership of television and radio stations to spread the cost of gathering news stories.

- Target marketing: the gathering of health-care articles in magazine form for resale to physicians for their waiting rooms.

- Newsletter publishing: the sale of special-interest articles to selected consumers.

The strategic buyer will *impute* its ability to multiply cash-flow and add its skills to your niche, but narrowly focused, business. It happens all the time, to the gratitude of owners who are fortunate enough to sell to large corporations.

It is more difficult to obtain a higher price from financial buyers who seek to leverage everything in the company. Rather than emphasize upside opportunities, which fall on the deaf ears of the cash-flow-conscious financial buyer, stress opportunities to slash expenses. Some of these include the following:

Management salaries

Management Perks

Space

Administrative Personnel

Vehicles

Lawyers

Auditors

Health Insurance

Commercial Insurance

Telephone

Postage

Courier

Travel and Entertainment

Advertising

It could mean a significant amount of money in your pocket to know in advance if your deal is either strategic or financial. Take the time to understand the difference up front.

HERE'S THE PROBLEM...HERE'S THE SOLUTION

The first step in deal closing is identifying the problem you hope to solve with your deal. Problems are markets in search of solutions. All successful deal closers have a unique ability to formulate problems. In economic terms this means identifying a market or a problem in search of a solution.

Here's a tip: *The first millionaire in any new market is the person who indexes problems and then sells the indexes to others.*

THE MICHAEL JORDAN CLOSING STRATEGY

When the incomparable basketball player Michael Jordan gets his hands on the ball and begins his magnificently choreographed drive to the basket, he attempts to *close a deal*—albeit, a two-point deal. But Jordan does it with such frequency, and with such a combination of unusual grace and skill never before seen in basketball, that his strategy is worth studying and emulating.

From his first step on the court, Jordan is problem formulating. He observes the placement of the defensive players, reflects briefly on what they are likely to do to try to stop him, observes mentally the location of his teammates and their practiced moves, then formulates his plan. Like all great closers, Jordan thinks *associationally* rather than *linearly*. Many people think in terms of straight lines; that is, you can get from here to there by taking one and only one path, and that path is the shortest, most direct route. An associational thinker sees many paths, some of them fairly circuitous, but all of them capable of getting the ball into the hoop, so to speak.

In thinking associationally while many of his opponents think linearly, Jordan scores more points than anyone else in the game, time after time. In so doing, the basket appears to be wider for Jordan. And that, as we shall see, is the goal of closing deals. Problem formulating in deal-making is assessing the number of paths upfront before the closing process begins.

Pyramidal Thinking

If basketball isn't your game, perhaps the concept of problem formulating may become clear if you replace the basketball imagery with that of a triangle or pyramid. The goal is the same: Widen the hoop or widen the top of the pyramid, to allow more scores—more closings.

As in basketball, so it is in deal closings. If the multiple channels are not captured and held by the team with the ball, the competition will take "the ball" and block the closer out of a particular market. Exhibit 1.1 shows how the pyramid appears to the deal closer who problem-formulates upfront.

Gloria Steinem, cofounder of *Ms.* magazine, is a successful entrepreneur. She problem-formulated brilliantly in the uncertain arena of women's liberation. Problems in this area have run the gamut from women not receiving equal pay for equal work, to sexual harassment on the job, to abortion, to new political agenda issues. A more complicated, multilevel problem area probably does not exist. Steinem realized that women's liberation problems simply needed to be *indexed*. What better way to sell an index to a market eager to learn more about women's liberation problems than through a magazine? Widely read magazines attract advertisers, and so the index would pay for itself. The first entrepreneur to attack a new problem usually becomes its *indexer*. Pat McGovern did this as well with software, in the publication *Computerworld*.

Steinem perceived that corporations would pay her to help them solve large problems dealing with women as customers. For example, truck drivers were increasingly becoming husband-and-wife teams in the 1970s, and the truck manufacturers wanted to learn more about designing a cab suitable for women. A $250,000 consulting contract from a major truck manufacturer has more profit potential than the

Exhibit 1.1
THE PYRAMID STRATEGY OF PROBLEM FORMULATING

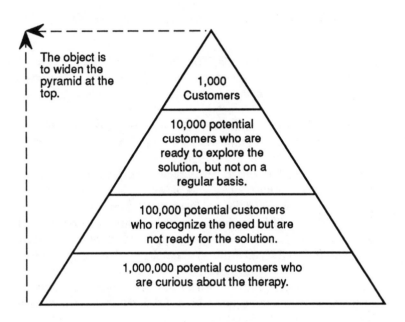

The object is to widen the pyramid at the top.

1,000 Customers

10,000 potential customers who are ready to explore the solution, but not on a regular basis.

100,000 potential customers who recognize the need but are not ready for the solution.

1,000,000 potential customers who are curious about the therapy.

sale of $250,000 worth of advertisements in the magazine, and Steinem recognized this.

Let us assume that the women's liberation market was not problem-formulated in detail, but, rather, that an entrepreneur began selling services to truck manufacturers to help them redesign cabs for a newly created female driver market. The entrepreneur in this instance creates the solution before identifying the market properly, and that puts the cart before the horse. The truck manufacturers would rebuff the entrepreneur in one of the following ways:

> I was not aware that we had the problem that you are describing.
>
> We would like some assistance in solving this problem, but how do we know you have developed the solution?
>
> We have the problem, you have the solution, but what credentials do you have in this field?

These three questions deal with three specific *lacks*: lack of information, lack of trust, and lack of credibility. Marketing professionals frequently know how to overcome these lacks, but entrepreneurs usually do not.

Many new business failures are the result of inadequate problem formulation. Entrepreneurs make this mistake less frequently, however, than do small business persons and large corporations. It is the plight of small business persons such as merchants to open stores with products that interest them and to locate them in convenient or available locations. Unfortunately, the market is not always interested. Large corporations rush solutions to the market and then try to use brute market leverage to place the product onto the shelves and spend millions of dollars in advertising, bleating "cheap, cheap, cheap," to move the product off the shelves, only to pull it completely following a few months of red ink. Feminine deodorant spray is an example of a $100 million solution to a nonproblem. "Real" cigarettes produced a $45 million loss for Reynolds Tobacco. Texas Instruments' home computer was too expensive. Topps Chewing Gum brought us chocolate bubble gum in 1980 to everyone's lack of interest. Even the mighty Xerox Corporation blew it in the personal computer market by selling dumb hardware instead of solutions-oriented software. According to the International Franchise Association, one reason that 95 percent of all franchised stores succeed for at least three years is that their franchisor problem formulates for them and writes out the solution-delivery method in long, detailed training-and-operations manuals.

Artists as Problem Formulators

The study of creativity among artists by Jacob Getzels and Mihaly Csikszentmihalyi has a bearing on our investigation of the deal-making process.*

The participants in the study were young male art students. Each participant first completed a still life for the researchers based on an arrangement from a collection of objects provided. Afterward, the artist answered several questions.

One question posed was: "Could any of the elements in your drawing be eliminated or altered without destroying its character?" The objective of the investigators was to determine whether or not a student considered his work "fixed" or "flexible."

The answers to this question enabled Getzels and Csikszentmihalyi to draw a correlation between *ability* and *recognition of the possibility of change*. A panel of judges rated each artist's drawing. Those who received the highest ratings overall were the ones who said their work might be changed. A follow-up study seven years later by the same investigators indicated that more success had come to the artists who earlier had seen the possibility for change.

Perfection is too costly to achieve. Rather than spending the time and effort to be perfect, a successful artist can spend less time and be satisfied. *Satisfaction* is the goal in problem finding, *not* perfection. The potential deal-maker should free his or her mind of any notions of finding the perfect problem and supplying that demand curve with a perfect solution. In the deal-making process, random collisions are the norm.

The most effective artists were found to have displayed these work traits: In arranging the objects that they were preparing to paint, they manipulated them more, moved them about and then rearranged them more, moved the mechanical parts more, and chose more unusual objects. They tended not to have a predetermined theme in mind prior to beginning to paint, but discovered arrangements through handling the objects.

---

* Jacob Getzels and Mihaly Csikszentmihalyi, *The Creative Vision: A Longitudinal Study of Problem Finding in Art*, New York: John Wiley & Sons, Inc., 1976.

As they began drawing, they more often rearranged or substituted objects, changed paper, switched media, and transformed the scene and subject of the drawing. The final structure of the drawing tended to emerge later rather than earlier. The researchers regarded the artists' problem finding as a measure of their creativity. The more creative artists, who indeed became more successful seven years later, devoted more time to problem formulation.

Even the late George Quist, a venture capitalist who began in the early 1970s providing seed capital to some of the most successful entrepreneurs in the country, said essentially the same thing: "The road to success isn't always going to be straight. The smart guy will realize there will be a lot of turns—changes in the market, for instance. The honest entrepreneur can face up to that."[*]

Random Collisions of Positive Factors

Ward Parkinson, founder of Micron Technology Corporation, beat all of the established American and Japanese semiconductor companies in the 1980s with the development of 64K DRAM chips. He ignored the elegant visions of chip design engineers and focused instead on providing as much space on the chip for memory as possible. For the personal computer, producing adequate memory capability is one of the biggest problems in need of a solution. His trial-and-error methods eventually led to the technological breakthrough that his former boss, L. J. Sevin, founder of Mostek Corporation, did not take advantage of.

William Benton sold his interest in the advertising agency Benton & Bowles in 1935 and, in his words, "began making money in mistakes."[**] Soon thereafter, Robert M. Hutchins hired Benton to do public relations for the University of Chicago. Benton knew that Sears, Roebuck & Company wanted to sell *Encyclopaedia Britannica* because it needed to be updated. He convinced Sears to donate it to the university, but he was unable to convince the university's

---

[*] "Do You Have What It Takes?", *Forbes*, August 3, 1961.
[**] Ibid.

trustees to pay to have the encyclopedia revised. Benton agreed to invest $100,000 to have it updated, for which he received two thirds of the stock. The encyclopedia has become a cash cow. Benton expanded the company by enfolding the Merriam-Webster Company in the mid-1950s.

The message is clear—find an interesting problem and carefully observe every aspect, because once it becomes the *raison d'etre* of your business, the various components of the problem will collide with one another and with other variables and force you to rearrange your business plan. Finding problems can be a relatively simple procedure, however.

The newspaper is one of the best sources of lift-off opportunities in the country. Large-city newspapers index the world's problems and serve potential deal-makers a banquet of opportunities.

Like bulky luggage on a long journey, problem formulation brings with it continual failure and frustration. If it comes too easily, some important component was probably overlooked. For instance, laser interactive videodiscs have left CBS and RCA Corporation bloodied and bowed, each emptying over $100 million in the field. Both CBS and RCA built the devices *without* software to make them "interesting." Rarely is the entrepreneur successful who launches a company without all the necessary capital, in this case, software. Rolm Corporation, which arguably developed the most efficiently automated telephone exchange, PABX systems, launched its product with $200,000 and struggled from 1964 to 1974. Ten years later, International Business Machines Corporation acquired Rolm for $1.8 billion.

CAPITALIZING ON BUREAUCRATIC INEFFICIENCY

Successful deal makers also find problems in services undertaken by the government but implemented poorly. Post offices are a case in point. You can set up a private post office near a U.S. Post Office and charge a premium for stamps and box rental. Your unique services would be speed and courtesy. You need only promise that the line of customers would never exceed two. If more than two people wait in line, another service person can come to the counter.

Scott Adler, a 35-year-old electrical engineer, opened several storefront post offices in the Los Angeles area in 1982, accepting packages for shipment by United Parcel Service, Federal Express, Trans-box, and the U.S. Postal Service. All services exact the normal fees. Several times a day, Adler's post offices turn their mail over to appropriate carriers. His handling fee is $1 to $5 per item, frequently greater than the postage cost. Adler's solution—to offer speed, convenience, and courtesy—is simple. His initial problem formulation was complex and unique.

Adler's post offices are in malls and near banks, places that people visit once a day. The closest U.S. Post Office is located out of the way in a cluster of government buildings noted for traffic snarls and insufficient parking. United Parcel Service and Federal Express require that the sender or receiver be home when they arrive; thus, people frequently prefer to take those kinds of packages to the courier. Adler's post office centralizes this function. His fee represents a savings in gasoline, driving time, and parking hassles. His post office idea can be replicated and should be franchised for speed of multimarket penetration. When it is, the U.S. Postal Service will be whittled down to an efficient, manageable size.

PROFITING ON SIMPLE EMOTIONS

Roger Horchow publishes a catalog chock-full of beautiful personal items—very expensive, and very chic. Others also publish handsome catalogs, but Horchow does it better. The problem that he has identified goes by many names, but has to do with simple vanity. People love themselves and every once in a while like to strut their stuff. So Roger Horchow has prepared a catalog for gift givers in which he encourages the customer to put the initials of the recipient on the gift. He knows that most people are too vain to return gifts that have their initials on them.

HEADLINE WRITING: WHAT SETS YOUR DEAL APART

What is the difference between your deal and others in the same industry or market sector? What single factor sets it apart? Whatever it may be, find it because it is your DEP factor. Don't look at the uniqueness of the product or service because that is probably not where it is. It is probably not in the nonduplicability of its service. It is probably not certain efficiencies within your company that will enhance profitability. These are some of the key factors that will enable your company or project to achieve its demonstrable economic justification and to compete effectively once it gets funded and up-and-running.

Premise

The key word is *proposition*. Your deal hasn't unfolded and been tested in the icy waters of the marketplace, so there is no proof that it will work. Therefore, its success is hypothetical. It depends on the size of the problem, or need, or opportunity that your solution is aimed at. Define the opportunity, or the problem for which your deal may be the solution, and you are halfway home in discovering the inescapable premise that will make customers line up in droves to buy your product. If you fail to discover and project the premise, buyers, in the inimitable words of Samuel Goldwyn describing a movie of his that flopped, "will stay away in droves."

Problem Awareness

The second half of the premise is to make as certain as possible that the customers who you believe have a problem for which you have a unique solution actually perceive the problem, are aware of the problem, and are willing to pay for a solution. There are many problems in society but often the people who share them do not recognize them as more than "their lot in life" or "that's just the way things are." They are resigned to their condition. They are reminiscent of the drivers who see the following sign that I once saw on a southern Georgia dirt road—"Pick your rut carefully because you're going to be in it for 40 miles"—and keep driving.

If people are not aware that they have a problem, they will not pay for its solution. The DeLorean automobile flopped for several reasons, one of which was that it didn't solve a need. It wasn't safer than any other car. It wasn't a car that evoked memories of the customers' happy teenage years. It wasn't handsomer, or sleeker, or more comfortable than competitive cars. It was a "me-too."

The Safe Car

As an aside, the question of whether or not customers will flock to a safe car, one in which passengers always survive a head-on collision at 55 miles per hour, is a burning issue. With the wellness phenomenon in full flower, with breakfast cereals being pushed as pharmaceuticals, and with the recent exposé that certain advertising agents falsified the safety features of their cars to make them appear safer, one would think that the American consumer is ready for the safe car. Technically, it can be built. And it can be built for less than an additional $5,000 by adapting a handful of features used in Indy race cars. Some of these include embedding the gasoline tank, the principal source of fires, in polystyrene; using foot-thick steel doors; placing the gasoline tank in the center of the car rather than in the rear; and adding double air bags, shatter-proof glass, and a steering mechanism that falls downward in the event of a head-on crash. The solution is available. The problem of highway deaths exists. But is there a demonstrable economic proposition? Is there a compelling need on the part of consumers to own a safe car?

Surely there is an entrepreneur, trained in automobile design in Detroit's factories, who believes that he or she can bring a completely safe car to the market for which consumers will beat a path to the dealers' doors.

But where's the rub? Why isn't the safe car in dealer showrooms? Extensive market research will demonstrate that everyone wants a safe car. Thus, market research proves the need, but does not say that people will act on that need. Traditional corporations will research propositions such as this to death. Entrepreneurs act on intuition, gainsaying research as nonessential.

A *deal closer* will launch the Safe Car Company someday by skirting the safety issue entirely as the central proposition and appealing to the buyers' "gut," instead of his mind. He or she will underwrite the automobile insurance on its cars at 60 percent below the going rate. The demonstrable economic proposition will be "the car for people who want to save thousands of dollars on their insurance." Because most people believe that their number won't come up in a car accident, the idea of buying a safe car is not compelling. But the idea of lowering the family's automobile insurance costs from $3,000 a year, for a family of four, to $900 a year is a compelling hypothesis. Corporate fleets, car rental companies, and heads of large households of drivers will find the premise terribly persuasive.

The point of the parable of the safe car is that no one believes their number will come up in a car wreck, but everyone would like to save on automobile insurance costs. Thus, the DEP factor is in a side issue, and not in the product itself.

The DEP Factor of Health Foods

Frequently, as in the case of the safe car example, the demonstrable economic proposition is not the most obvious factor. It is frequently a peripheral issue. For example, several entrepreneurs have launched health food companies in the last decade, and their products have gone platinum—literally leapt off the supermarket shelves and into the shoppers' bags. Yet few people have seen their advertisements because the companies are capitalized too thinly to afford any. New Morning breakfast cereal is capturing eye-level shelf space in supermarkets in New England and other regions. Cholesterol-free Saratoga Potato Chips is a top seller in New York metropolitan area supermarkets. Both products are demonstrably healthier than conventional breakfast cereals and potato chips, but they have not spent meaningful advertising dollars trying to position their products as quasipharmaceuticals as have certain cereal manufacturers such as Quaker Oats.

New Morning and Saratoga have developed unique distribution systems and coupled them with massive public relations in which health and food writers praise their products. Consumers clip the articles and walk into their neighborhood supermarkets and demand them. The store manager may be out of the products the first time Mr. Shopper, who has a family of five and who spends $150 per week at the store, asks for the product. But she won't be out of it the second time.

The store manager asks New Morning and Saratoga to accept two feet of shelf space for their products free of charge, at eye level. That's known as "shunning the pike," or avoiding the tollgate. Whereas nearly every food processor, from the largest to the smallest, must pay slotting allowances of not insignificant amounts to supermarkets so as to introduce new products, the demonstrable economic proposition that New Morning and Saratoga have made is that they avoid these tolls with consumer demand; or as it is sometimes called, *consumer pull-through.*

The savings in advertising dollars and slotting allowances enables these and other new health food processors to one-up the majors who, in their usual "throw money at the problem" marketing strategy, are trying to make pharmacological claims for oatmeal and other cereals with six-figure prime-time television spots and are losing market share for their trouble.

When a product has an established market following, as does oatmeal, to try to reposition it as a pharmaceutical—as a food product that lowers the risk of contracting colon cancer—is foolhardy. Why not come out with a new Quaker-developed health food product and compete with yourself, rather than let New Morning capture the healthy segment of the market—especially when New Morning is a start-up with one millionth of Quaker's available capital? But people in large corporations frequently do not think strategically. They have the luxury of too much money and massive advertising budgets to think of innovative ways to leverage store managers into giving them two feet of absolutely free eye-level shelf space.

Saratoga Potato Chips

Daniel Feld, a former executive with Grey Advertising, left the buttoned-down world of Madison Avenue to launch a new potato chip manufacturer. The *premise of the product* is that the Saratoga potato chip is 100 percent cholesterol-free. Its secondary premise is that it is made in the Bronx, New York, and thus a consumer who buys Saratoga rather than Lay's, the number-one seller owned by the Frito-Lay division of Pepsico, is helping to increase employment in the Bronx. Its tertiary premise is that it is a "regional" product, somehow designed to appeal to the palates of New Yorkers. These are the premises of the product—what I have referred to as its *solutions* to consumer problems.

The DEP factor of Saratoga Potato Chip Corporation is different, and knowing the distinction is key to how Dan Feld closes deals for shelf space in supermarkets throughout the northeast and thus attracts start-up capital.

There are four steps in Feld's strategy:

1. Create a product that is healthier than existing products, thus making them no substitute for yours, while making yours a substitute for all others.

2. Generate authoritative and positive product reviews and endorsements from significant widely-read newspapers and journals, to create consumer awareness, demand, and pull-through.

3. Ask store managers for eye-level shelf space—or air space, such as end-of-aisle containers that have not been producing revenue for the store—and in return, you will create a health food "center" for them and take the buying hassle off their hands.

4. Persuade other health food producers to let you distribute for them, under their label or yours, and for a commission payable to you; they will be able to obtain eye level shelf space in every supermarket whose tollgate you have managed to jump.

Centrifugal Thinking

Take your eye off the uniqueness of your products. That is centripetal thinking. Put your eye on the problem that you are solving for consumers. Begin with the question: If consumers want healthier foods, how do I get health food products in front of them in stores where they regularly shop? The answer: Provide authoritative information that creates product awareness and consumer pull-through.

Thus, the DEP factor of the Saratoga Potato Chip Corporation is not found in the uniqueness of the product or the jobs that are created with each crunchy bite. It is found in the company's product-distribution system.

Movie distribution, as well, is a clogged channel that entrepreneurs, known in this industry as independent movie producers, find overwhelmingly difficult to get started in. Strategies for jumping the tollgates in the movie industry will be described and explained in Chapter 3: How to Get Past the Gatekeepers.

2

TARGETING PROSPECTIVE BUYERS

FINDING COOPERATIVE BUYERS: THE LAW OF RECIPROCITY

The overriding, unspoken rule in business is trust—the knowledge inherent in all business people that they may meet again and that if a person has gone back on his or her word, he or she cannot be trusted the next time around. This is the *Law of Reciprocity:* Achievement is rewarded, failure is punished, and dishonesty results in banishment. Cooperation *is* deal-making, and it goes well when all the parties understand the Law of Reciprocity.

The best way to ensure cooperation from your buyer is always do what you say you will do and be very clear upfront. Failure to deliver on a promise is tantamount to asking not to be trusted.

If you don't obtain permission upfront, you will have to ask for forgiveness later on. And forgiveness is sometimes extremely expensive; read "litigation." These rules apply to the buyer of the deal as well as to the seller. For example, a buyer who fails to show up for meetings or who is late for meetings or who continually takes telephone calls while you are trying to present your deal or who attempts through word and deed to gain the upper hand in a deal discussion by setting up hurdles, detours, and orange cones in the road, is probably not going to be someone who will *cooperate* well with you after the deal is struck.

THE AXELROD SOLUTION: CLARIFY UPFRONT

Interdependence means that those in business must cooperate with one another selectively. According to Robert Axelrod (*The Evolution of Cooperation*, New York: Basic Books, 1984, p. 3), people can and will evolve reliable cooperative strategies in totally selfish environments. Axelrod sought to answer a fundamental question:

> Under what conditions will cooperation emerge in a world of egoists without central authority? This question intrigued people for a long time. And for good reason. We all know that people are not angels, and that they tend to look after themselves and their own first. Yet we also know that cooperation does occur and that our civilization is based upon it.

In 1979, Axelrod sent out invitations to hundreds of game theorists telling them to pit their strategies against one another in a round-robin Prisoner's Dilemma tournament, with the overall goal of amassing the most points. The Prisoner's Dilemma game has two players, each of whom has two choices, namely, *cooperate* or *defect*. Each must make the choice not knowing what the other will do. No matter what the other does, defection yields a higher payoff than cooperation does. The dilemma is that if both defect, both do worse than if both had cooperated.

A metaphor for the Prisoner's Dilemma would be the case of the two industrial nations that have erected trade barriers to each other's exports. Because of the mutual advantages of free trade, both countries would be better off if these barriers were eliminated. But if either country were to eliminate its barriers unilaterally, it would find itself facing terms of trade that hurt its own economy. In fact, whatever one country does, the other country is better off retaining its trade barriers.

The winning strategy in Axelrod's Prisoner's Dilemma game is basic tit-for-tat. Tactics are as follows: Cooperate on the first move; thereafter, do whatever the other player did on the previous move. If it cooperated, then you cooperate. If it defected, then you defect, but be willing to forgive if it agrees to cooperate and return to a cooperative strategy.

Axelrod adds that with *clarity* upfront—telling your opponent that your strategy will be to cooperate, but if defected against, you will defect until the opponent returns to a cooperative strategy—selfish competitors can evolve to higher levels of homeostasis in their marketplaces. Be certain that you ask if your opponent understands your position clearly.

Shareware: Cooperation in Action

In 1987, Quicksoft Corporation, a small Seattle-based computer software developer founded by Robert Wallace, made the following offer to consumers at a computer expo: Try the software. If you like it, send Quicksoft $75. If you don't like it, don't pay. The catch is that if you like it and don't pay (Axelrod's defection), you don't get the follow-on disks that contain the most advanced applications. Satisfied customers such as Times-Mirror, Caterpillar, and DuPont have sent the company over $10 million in payments.

Shareware vendors, especially ones that lack money for advertising, have discovered a road around the software retailer. ButtonWare, a Bellevue, Washington, software producer, sells its product, PC-File, via shareware. Its sales in 1990 were $8 million. A third vendor, Magee Enterprises of Atlanta, Georgia, achieved sales of $5 million in 1990 for its product Automenu.

The originator of shareware, Andrew Fluegelman, was founding editor of *PC World*. He called shareware an "experiment in economics." Software products are less expensive (that is, no advertising) if marketed via shareware. Quicksoft's PC-Write costs the consumer $89 and does just about everything that MicroPro's $495 Wordstar package does. With shareware, for a small membership fee, the consumer can ask questions of the vendor via electronic mail.

Herb Boulden, project analyst for the Rockwell International Electronics Group in Anaheim, California, is a shareware fan. Boulden's job is to service three thousand personal computers for more than nine thousand Rockwell employees on the West Coast. He likes the support that Quicksoft provides to thousands of shareware users.

Cindy Kear, editor of *Shareware*, reports that it has as many as one hundred thousand readers and that its function is to review products and to inform the reader which software is legitimate and which has been cooked up by a hacker in his kitchen without suitable testing or documentation to support customers. Ms. Kear told me that about six hundred new software products come into the shareware market each year from programmers and that her tollgate determines whether or not PC users can rely on their creators for after-sale support.

Walter Kennamer, partner in charge of Ernst & Young's microcomputer support, has ordered over ten thousand copies of shareware for his firm's worldwide offices. Shareware vendors spend very little on advertising and can earn a reasonable profit with product prices under $100 plus a membership fee for support services.

STRIVE FOR TRANSACTIONS, NOT RELATIONSHIPS

The purpose of business is to make your product or service a substitute for all other competitive products and services and to make all other products and services no substitute for yours. The buyer is sovereign; it is his or her demand for your product or service, or those of competitive products or services, that creates a marketplace. Your product is valued for the satisfaction it provides to someone. The greater the perceived value, the greater the profit. And the greater the number of someones who perceive its value, the more wealth you will create.

If you are in business for any reason other than that which I have just stated, there is a very likely chance you will fail. *Let there be no substitute* for what you do should be the phrase chiseled in marble on your desk. If not, who would want to do business with you?

It seems that every large service corporation is proclaiming in advertisements that it is in the *relationship* and not the *transaction* business. Most of these disquisitions are from commercial banks that have been the effective agents of some of the sorriest transactions in commercial banking history: real estate loans based on appraisals bid up by excessive property buys; junk bond loans to raiders who can transact but can't manage; and loans to foreign governments whose leaders can neither transact nor manage.

Relationship business means getting to know your client intimately through in-depth analysis and due diligence. Service providers overemphasized transactions and underemphasized relationships in the 1980s.

Don't let the ads fool you. Relationships are marriages; transactions are affairs. Business deals are affairs; marriages are for the home. Thus, the transaction is first and foremost, and if positive relationships grow out of them that is a plus, but not the critical issue. Transactions—closings—are the spark that ignites the engines of business.

Most people forget the need to make their deal a *substitute* for all others, and most people believe that they must bond with the buyer rather than *transact* with her.

We learn from our mistakes, but the lessons are costly. It is less expensive to learn from the mistakes of others. Let's take a look at the winding path to a difficult closing taken by the inventor of one of the most revolutionary products in the history of our civilization: the Xerox machine. It took him longer to find a backer for his device than it took Christopher Columbus 450 years before him to finance a trip from Spain to the New World.

The Odyssey of Xerography

Chester Carlson, the inventor of xerography, was like the first person who ate a lobster and then tried to persuade others that the funny-looking crustacean was *food*. It must have been a tough proposition to persuade investors and buyers that xerography had utility and validity. Carlson was, in the early 1950s, trying to sell xerography against the highly popular mimeograph system. Mimeography was slow, messy, inefficient, difficult to correct errors on, and fairly expensive, but large office-equipment manufacturing firms had important sums of money invested in it and did not wish to make capital-draining changes.

A patent attorney by profession, Carlson initially saw a myopic use for xerography as a means only of reproducing blueprints. A tall, craggy, slightly stooped man who wore a tan raincoat and a weathered hat, Carlson would trudge from corporation to corporation to seek a sponsor and seed capital. He went to Eastman Kodak, Bell and Howell, IBM, and GAF to demonstrate in a rudimentary fashion the fundamentals of xerography. None expressed an interest in Carlson's invention.

With one hand he would reach into a raincoat pocket and pull out a small piece of stainless steel. From an inside jacket pocket he would remove a piece of typewritten paper. Then he would dive into another pocket and pull out a rabbit's foot. He would take the rabbit's foot and polish the little bar of stainless steel vigorously. When it was polished, he would reach into another pocket and pull out a small container of powder. He would sprinkle the powder on a plain piece of paper and hold it, the stainless steel, and the typewritten paper up against a light. In a few minutes, the words on the typewritten paper would be transferred to the plain piece of paper.

"This method that Mr. Carlson is showing us will never replace the mimeograph machine," said the corporate planning officers of the major office-equipment manufacturers. The venerable Arthur D. Little consulting firm was so bold as to put its strongly worded negative appraisal in writing.

After several years of show-and-tell in search of a deal, Chester Carlson met Joseph Wilson, a young man just returned from the Korean War whose family had recently turned over to him the Haloid Company to manage. Haloid, a manufacturer of mimeograph paper, had annual sales of $6 million but was not growing. Wilson was looking for new product ideas that did not require a lot of money to develop. He consulted with Haloid's lawyer, Sol Linowitz.

Jointly, the two decided that if an engineering firm could build a production model of the machine to carry out Carlson's patent design, and if the machine could then be manufactured for a reasonable cost, Haloid would acquire Carlson's rights in exchange for Haloid stock and finance the product launch. A small engineering and consulting firm in Columbus, Ohio, called Battelle, agreed to take on the engineering assignment. Haloid could not pay Battelle's fee. Happily, the engineering firm was willing to take its payment in stock. The rest of the story is fairly well known. Carlson received stock that became worth around $100 million, Battelle became a very well-known research organization, and the University of Rochester, an early investor, built the third largest endowment among all universities in the United States. Corporations began purchasing the first Xerox machines, which became so popular that personnel reproduced their books, menus, and birth certificates ad nauseum to the point that the early Xerox machines needed guards. Haloid changed its name to Xerox Corporation, and one of the most successful companies of the last 25 years was launched.

Carlson's Selling Mistakes

There are six steps in the closing process, and Carlson missed them all.

1. He misunderstood xerography's demonstrable proposition, assuming it solved problems associated with duplicating blueprints only. The copying of blueprints represented an insignificant market.

2. He sought capital from corporations that were highly unlikely to invest because they were protecting vested interests.

3. Eastman Kodak, IBM, Bell and Howell, GAF and others did not wish to see any innovations in their existing duplicating-equipment markets. Not until Carlson met Haloid, who brought in Batelle, did he implement a strategy for end-running the "toll-gates" erected by the established companies.

4. Carlson did not create a community of interested parties in which others beside himself would have something of value to lose if a deal to launch xerography did not close. Late in the game Wilson and Linowitz began to spend some important money,

and they brought in Battelle, which, along with Haloid, had
something to lose if xerography failed to launch.

5. Carlson demonstrated the mechanics of xerography to target buyers
   when closing a deal requires asking questions of prospective
   buyers as to how they perceive their problem and what features
   a solution might have.

6. The endorsement of xerography via the Battelle imprimatur was
   brought to bear in the eleventh hour. Closing a deal requires
   third-party endorsement from an impeccable, independent source.

It is a stunning irony that one of the most significant breakthroughs
in the history of civilization was rejected by nearly every corporation
to which it was presented and took more than a decade from conception
to launch.

You would be surprised how many people use the Carlson closing
procedure today and give up the chase because of rejection. They
major in minors: the "uniqueness" of the project in their eyes, without
proper regard for the needs of buyers.

THE PROS AND CONS
OF BUYER-FINANCED DEALS

Service companies are unique in two respects: (1) many entrepreneurs
are attracted to the idea of starting service companies, and (2) it is
very difficult to raise serious amounts of capital for them. Venture
capitalists have protested that the problem with service companies
is that the "assets" go home every night and may not return. Thus,
service company entrepreneurs, lacking the enormous sums of start-up
capital lavished on their fellow entrepreneurs who have tires to kick,
have in desperation come up with unique financing methods. Coin-
cidentally, sources of capital come from the people with the problem;
that is, customer financing. Approximately 20 percent of the greatest
entrepreneurs of the last 25 years relied on buyer financing for their
launch capital. A substantial number of successful service companies
have been customer financed because it occurred to the deal-makers

that their customers could be persuaded to risk capital upfront. The insurance industry was launched with customer financing. Many customer-financed companies are well known and include Arthur Murray Dance Studios, Weight Watchers International, Century 21 Real Estate, EST, Book-of-the-Month Club, Evelyn Wood Reading Dynamics, Pizza Hut, ComputerLand Corporation, CMP Communications, Renovators Supply, Mary Kay Cosmetics, Avon Products, Shaklee, Time, Maxicare, and others. The primary forms of customer financing are the following:

Franchising

Facilities Management

Newsletters

Seminars

Direct Mail Marketing

Licensing

Consulting

Party Plan Selling

The advantages to buyer financing are that it preserves equity for the founders; it involves the customer in developing the solution to the problem directly; and it is a faster means of raising capital than making presentations to investors and their attorneys. The disadvantage to buyer financing is that there must be no delay in delivering the service or product that the customer has paid for in advance. Thus, the entrepreneur must prepare the product or service in advance in order to be ready to deliver it within 60 days of receiving payment. Society benefits because the customer is involved with the development of an appropriate cost-effective solution to the problem that saves time, and venture capital is conserved for more capital-intensive projects. An exhaustive problem-formulation process can be less painful and anguished if the entrepreneur analyzes various forms of customer financing first, to see if the problem is large enough to warrant advance payment to finance a solution.

TEN SUCCESSFUL ENTREPRENEURIAL COMPANIES

Companies   *DEP Factor*

1. Wal-Mart Stores, Inc
   Founder: Samuel Moore
   Walton
   Founded: 1962
   Location: Bentonville, AR
   Wealth Created: $12 billion

People in small towns (under 5,000 pop.) were being exposed to vast arrays of general merchandise on television at discount prices but the nearest stores to them were several hundred miles away. Walton figured the big competitors—K-Mart, Newberry, TG&Y, Gibson's, and others—would ignore him if he concentrated on small towns. They did, and Wal-Mart passed them by to become the largest retailer in the world in less than 30 years.

2. McDonalds Corporation
   Founder: Raymond A. Kroc
   Founded: 1961
   Location: Northbrook, IL
   Wealth Created: $4.2 billion

Kroc observed in the late 1950s that wives were beginning to join the work force along with their husbands (or were part of a growing number of single-parent households) that created a trend toward eating more dinners out. However, drive-ins were too dirty and noisy to attract families. He created a chain of clean, sit-down, fast-food hamburger restaurants that working women could recommend to their families as reliable, attractive, and nearby.

3. Federal Express Corporation
   Founder: Frederick W. Smith
   Founded: 1973
   Location: Memphis, TN
   Wealth Created: $1.7 billion

The premise that Smith described in a paper for an economics course at Yale University was that the existing means for delivering packages overnight was unreliable and expensive. Air freight companies shipped their clients' packages on commercial airplanes; and if weather or equipment problems prevented takeoffs or landings, the packages did not get shipped. Smith introduced a small-package and urgent-document transportation system. Although he received a grade of C on his term paper, the customers of Federal Express have learned to rely with confidence on the arrival of their packages the next day.

4. Rouse Company
   Founder: James W. Rouse
   Founded: 1939
   Location: Columbia, MD
   Wealth Created: $495 million

Rouse identified urban blight and decay as a problem capable of entrepreneurial solution. He developed the know-how to pull together capital, local government support, and the sweat equity of the urban poor to rebuild blighted urban areas into festivals of small shops, exciting restaurants and outdoor markets, and clean, safe living areas. Fanueil Hall in Boston and the South Street Seaport in New York City are proof that Rouse's hypothesis was correct.

5. Liz Claiborne, Inc.
   Founder: Elisabeth Claiborne Ortenberg
   Founded: 1976
   Location: New York, NY
   Wealth Created: $347 million

Ms. Ortenberg observed a massive influx of young women into professions once the province of men— law, investment and commercial banking, advertising, and management. Their need was to wear well-made, fashionable sportswear to the office. But they were too busy to shop, so they shopped in department stores to be certain of getting quality and service. Ms. Ortenberg developed a designer label and trained department store salespersons in how to sell and service her line to busy, intelligent, on-the-go women.

6. Sea-Land Services, Inc.
   Founder: Malcom P. McLean
   Founded: 1961
   Location: Port Elizabeth, NJ
   Wealth Created: $600 million

McLean observed that a large percentage of liquor shipped from Europe in barrels stacked in the hulls of ships was not making it to American bottlers. The barrels were being pilfered at the dock. McLean conceived the idea of shipping products in sealed containers, the same ones that fit onto the backs of trucks. To do this, he bought mothballed ships used during World War II and put "honeycombs" into their hulls to hold truck containers. McLean's solution has helped to hold down the cost of imported products.

7. MCI Communications
   Corporation
   Founder:
   William G. McGowan
   Founded: 1968
   Location: Washington, DC
   Wealth Created: $2.8 billion

McGowan observed that AT&T was gouging the public with monopolistic prices on telephone rentals, long-distance calls, and poor customer service. He challenged the monopoly with a microwave voice communication link between Chicago and St. Louis that was one half the price charged by AT&T. He attracted lots of customers; AT&T sued, but lost and had to begin lowering its rates to remain competitive with MCI and its clones.

8. Lucasfilms, Inc.
   Founder: George Lucas
   Founded: 1975
   Location: Lucas Valley, CA
   Wealth Created:
   Over $500 million

Lucas discovered a subject matter that appealed to the greatest number of movie goers: chase films that blended high technology—computer-controlled space ships—with high touch—warm, fuzzy animal creatures and humorous robots. Lucas' films introduced the concept of blockbuster films, ones that gross more than $100 million at the box-office, a similar amount in home video rentals, and a third cash flow channel from product sales—unheard of until the *Star Wars* saga.

9. NIKE, Inc.
   Founder: Philip H. Knight
   Founded: 1972
   Location: Beaverton, OR
   Wealth Created: $937 million

Knight formulated the problem in 1963 in a student term paper: With the demographic shift toward health care and physical fitness, more people would be running, or at least, walking. They would become conscious of what the professional athletes were wearing and seek to emulate them. Thus, if Knight could produce a high-quality, low-cost shoe endorsed by professional athletes, he would open up a mass market.

10. Honda Motor Company, Ltd.
    Founder: Soichiro Honda
    Founded: 1948
    Location: Tokyo, Japan
    Wealth Created: $9.4 billion

Honda broadened the marketplace for motorcycles by convincing "nice people" to buy them. He designed a step-through bike that combined the power and excitement of big machines with the convenience and efficiency of scooters and priced it well below the competition.

Honda's brilliant ad, "You meet
the nicest people on a Honda," gave
its motorbike mass market appeal.
The customers were subsequently
upgraded to Honda automobile
buyers.

These are 10 of the greatest entrepreneurial success stories of
all time, but each of them begins with a naive, simplistic premise.
If you are searching for a deal that you can call your own, look
around you at your community's problems and needs. Examine the
need that fits your abilities and areas of interest. Sketch some possible
solutions on a piece of paper using the pyramid method. Slowly but
surely the premise will appear, and from that base you can begin
thinking in terms of the sources of deal money, packaging the solution,
and closing strategies.

USING COUPONS TO TARGET NONCUSTOMERS

Isn't it amazing that consumer products companies offer coupons,
or product discounts, to their existing customers? When I open a
can of Folgers coffee I see a coupon imbedded in the coffee entitling
me to receive 30 cents off the next can of Folgers coffee I buy.
But why offer me, a Folgers' customer, a discount since I'm already
a customer willing to pay full price? In this case, couponing is a
waste of money.

Before there was a semiconductor to store the names of 90
million households, noncustomers were *promoted* with coupons. In
1968, approximately 16.5 billion coupons tumbled out of Sunday
newspapers, and roughly 10 percent of them were redeemed. In 1988,
221.7 billion coupons tumbled out of Sunday newspapers, but only
3.2 percent were redeemed. Furthermore, the majority of the redemp-
tions—80 percent by some estimates—were by loyal customers. Vendors
do not need to find and promote loyal customers with cents-off

coupons, but traditional marketing strategies are seemingly locked in. When couponing results in giving discounts to your customers 80 percent of the time, why bother with the cost of couponing? Why not simply lower prices? One answer is that people like to feel they are getting a deal.

The noncustomer is more important than the customer because the customer is already on your balance sheet, in your pocket, in the bank. The noncustomer is your challenge, the target of your intelligence, the prize in the game we call the competitive marketplace. If there weren't any noncustomers, business would be boring. There would be no competitor to leverage with a crafty marketing strategy. There would be no prize to reach for, no victory of increased market share, and no chase.

Look at all the business people who fake it. Look at all the money spent on marketing to customers when the contest, particularly in saturated markets, is who can take market share from the other guy. Any form of marketing that relies on conjecture or assumptions about what your noncustomer may or may not be thinking is faking it.

A computer chip can collect and store data on 75 million households, and this data is readily gatherable through R. L. Polk, census data, direct response, and telemarketing. Why, then, do large corporations pay their leaders millions of dollars per year to continue to put 221.7 billion coupons into Sunday newspapers when only 3.2 percent are redeemed, and 80 percent of those by loyal customers?

There are many points along the marketing highway where traditionally managed and deal-maker-managed companies diverge. But no single point of divergence is as dramatic as the traditionally managed company's strategy of selling to its customers and the deal-maker-managed company's strategy of selling to noncustomers. To the former, the customer is king. To the latter, *the noncustomer is king.* Since a typical company has 20 to 200 times more noncustomers than customers, which company is going to gain more market share in two to three years? The one that captures noncustomers. How is it going to do it? By making its noncustomers a deal, a bargain—*a demonstrable economic proposition.*

GATHERING INFORMATION ON NONBUYERS

The person you want to close is your nonbuyer. If the person is your buyer, then you have already closed him or her. If you sell a standardized nontailor-made, off-the-rack product or service, then the kind and amount of information that you need to gather is quite a bit different than if your product or service is customized. For the standardized product or service you will probably want to know the address, gender, age, family size, and telephone number of the buyer and who does the shopping.

You will want to compare this with similar information about your buyer to determine why you can close one group and not another. Thus, there are really two assignments to undertake when you set out to gather information on your nonbuyers:

1. Who are your buyers, where do they live, what are their genders, their ages, their family sizes, and who shops for your products or services?

2. Who are your nonbuyers, how do their demographics differ from your buyers, and how can you close them without losing your buyer base?

The means for gathering data on your buyers (if you have any) and on your nonbuyers is not difficult, although it is not done as frequently as one might imagine.

Closing Strategies for Car Dealers

There are roughly $550 of advertising costs for every car sold at retail. This number is derived by dividing annual unit car sales into annual automobile advertising by dealers. It does not include the annual advertising expenditures by automobile manufacturers. We also know from industry research that approximately one in five people who walk into an automobile showroom actually buy a car. Thus, if a typical car dealership sells 300 cars per year, it has spent $165,000 in advertising ($550 times 300); but, it has walked 1,200 potential customers: the four out of five who did not buy. Wouldn't it be smarter to focus the $165,000 advertising budget on the 1,200 non-customers and sell 900 cars per year rather than run generic ads and sell only 300 cars per year?

That is the premise of an up-start database marketing firm in Los Angeles named Lexi International, Inc. founded in 1987 by Robin D. Richards, 36, whose mission was to find noncustomers for consumer products companies and convert them into customers.

"We tripled the sales of a Hollywood, California, car dealer," says Richards. "We took one fifth of their annual advertising budget—about $40,000—and showed them how to close three out of five walk-ins; whereas before, using newspaper, radio, and television ads, they were closing one out of five."

Lexi's approach is made possible by use of a personal computer. First, it gathers information on all car registrations in the trading area of its client dealerships. It collects the names and addresses of people who own the make of car sold by its dealer as well as those that are directly price competitive. For instance, if its client is an Acura dealer, it collects names, addresses, and car registration data on Acura, Mercedes, and BMW owners in the trade area. All this information is available publicly. From published directories, Lexi can ascertain the trade-in value of every car in its databank.

Next, Lexi presents to its client the names of all owners of cars in its client's trade area who own a car that its client sells, but who bought it at another dealership outside the marketplace shared by the dealer and the car owner. Lexi's researchers have found that people frequently buy cars based on the reliability of the service department. That is, they may buy a Mercedes from a dealer near their home or place of business, but either receive poor mechanical service there and go elsewhere for service, or begin going elsewhere for service by happenstance and buy their next Mercedes at the dealer whose service department pleases them.

Third, Lexi's research team sorts through publicly available data on noncustomer owners of competitive cars in its client's trading area to learn as much about them as possible. For instance, car registration and census data both provide addresses as well as lots of other information about the people who inhabit those addresses.

A carefully written questionnaire is prepared. Lexi's telemarketers then telephone the noncustomers and conduct market research about why they buy a certain car, where they buy it, what they like about the car and their present dealer, and so forth. The telemarketers key the responses into their personal computers, and a software program analyzes the responses. A print-out on a particular noncustomer may include some of the following key factors:

> She originally bought cars from you but left four years ago when your service department changed the dial on the car's radio from the classical station that she always listens to to a Spanish music station.

> She used the word "engineering" five times in the interview.

> She particularly likes the way the car corners.

> She likes its weight and its heavy feeling, and she associates that with safety.

> When a dealer quotes her a price, she expects the dealer to stick to his word. Any deviation, and she will walk out.

There can be as many as 80 pieces of background data on a noncustomer that Lexi turns over to its car-dealer client in a thick notebook, the cost of which is considerably less than the $550 per person that the dealer spends on advertising.

This is pertinent research, but how does Lexi get the noncustomers to come into the dealership? It invites them to visit with a personalized engraved invitation. The invitation has a date and a time, and this date and time are tentatively agreed to on the telephone, during the course of the telemarketing interview. The engraved invitation formally reconfirms the appointment. In that most people have never been treated respectfully by a car dealer, they attend. A telephone reminder to reconfirm is the sealer.

From the moment the noncustomer walks into the dealership, the salesperson has him or her in his cross-hairs. Escape from a closing is nearly impossible if the salesperson carefully studied the Lexi noncustomer profile. As the salesperson knew what day and time of day the noncustomer was arriving, there was ample time to read the research report and prepare for the visit.

Is there any valid reason to use a "shotgun" approach to find automobile customers when shooting with a rifle—the chip—is so much more effective? Lexi International offers car dealers the ticket to closing more sales: Know your noncustomer.

CLOSING ONE-ON-ONE: DO YOUR RESEARCH FIRST

The same principles apply when you have to close one person only: Do your research. The noncustomer is now your target buyer. And the game isn't 10 car salespeople addressing 1,000 potential buyers. It's one-on-one basketball. The target buyer is the gatekeeper. Find his or her key, and he or she will open the tollgate and raise the bar.

If the gatekeeper is a well-known person, there may have been articles written about him or her. If not, but if the target buyer works for a publicly-owned company, there is likely to be information on him or her in a public filing with the Securities and Exchange Commission. You can order copies of prospectuses from Disclosure, Inc. by calling 1-800-638-8241, or you can order them from the publicly-held company itself.

Directories

There are directories available for nearly every industry, and if the target buyer works for a private company, it is likely that his name and other information appears in one or more of these directories. A big-city library will have many of these directories in its reference section. Dun & Bradstreet is the principal collector of data in the country. You can subscribe to one or more of its directories or to its report services; or if your budget will not permit a subscription, you can ask your banker or accountant to obtain a D&B report for you.

Titles

If your target buyer's name and background information is reported in the D&B report, you are fortunate because you will probably learn his or her age, title, rank in the company hierarchy, years with the company, previous position, and name and dates of college attended, if any. Titles can be deceptive. Generally, the people furthest removed from making buying decisions are those with the titles *Secretary, Treasurer,* and *Controller.* These people generally have administrative responsibilities such as personnel, insurance, accounts receivable collection, bank depository relationships, record-keeping, and report-filing functions with regulatory agencies. The title *Vice President,* on the other hand, generally means that the person can commit the company to a purchase order.

Commercial bank titles can be deceptive. The larger the title the greater the size of the loan that the individual can make on his or her initiation. The title *Cashier* is frequently used for a junior loan officer; sometimes the title *Assistant Treasurer* is used at the same level. This loan officer may be able to approve a loan of up to $25,000 on his or her own signature if it is in his or her area of responsibility. A more prestigious title, such as *Assistant Vice President,* generally means greater lending authority, perhaps up to $100,000, and so it goes up to *President.* Large loan requests (and every bank defines "large" differently) require loan committee approval. The same applies to nonbank lending institutions such as asset-based lenders and insurance companies.

A thorough and accurate directory will generally provide you with a snapshot of the hierarchy of decision makers at the buyer's company. If the person you are attempting to sell to is far down on the totem pole, or not listed at all, his or her ability to make a buying decision is probably slim. You may be able to close him or her, only to hear the response: "I certainly like what I've heard, but I don't have the authority to make a decision. You'll have to see my boss, and she's not in today, and I don't know when she can see you." Try to guage whom you are dealing with up front.

The CEO's Secretary

If you are not a subscriber to Dun & Bradstreet's reporting service, a single report will cost you around $200. However, most banks and large accounting firms are subscribers and can order a company report for you, and you will be able to see the names of the key officers and their backgrounds. If this is enough for you to determine which person in the organization has the authority to buy what you are selling, then you can focus in on that person. If not, then telephone the Chief Executive Officer and ask his or her secretary who is responsible for making decisions on whatever it is you are proposing.

When you want an answer to a question, and you want to learn something about your target buyer, always go to the top. This means the CEO's secretary when you are cold-calling or prospecting, as it is sometimes referred to. One of H. Ross Perot's greatest assets was doing research on target buyers before he made a sales call. Tom Spain, IBM's district manager in Dallas, and Perot's boss, said Perot was not a born salesperson. He had all the skills but he was too intense.

"He would literally isolate himself and study," Spain said. "When he came out of isolation he knew as much about the company or individual as anybody."[*] The place to begin studying is the CEO's secretary. He or she will know the importance of delegating responsibility to the right spot in the organization. If he or she does not know the name of the person to whom you should speak, you will not be switched to the personnel department (usually a dead end). You will most likely be put on hold while he or she asks someone in the senior executives' area for the name of the person you are seeking.

Ask for the correct spelling of the person's name. Everyone appreciates having their name spelled correctly. Also ask for the person's title, what building or floor they work in or on, and the name of the division or department that this person is a part of. The secretary may also be willing to tell you the name of the Department Head and title—the person that your target buyer may have to present your story to and someone whom you may subsequently have to sell once you get around the gatekeeper.

Having the name of the Department Head, you can perhaps gather what his or her other responsibilities are. He or she may

---

[*] Mason, Todd, *Perot: An Unauthorized Biography,* Dow Jones-Irwin, Homewood, Illinois, 1990, pp. 37–38.

have three or more areas of responsibility, such as Finance, Corporate Development, and New Product Research and Development. This could indicate three different sources of cash to apply toward innovation, new ventures, and acquisitions. Perhaps one source has more funds in it than another. A search of the available published information on the company may indicate the directions it is heading in and the opportunities it sees for itself.

Trade Journals

Every industry and most niches within industries have trade journals and newsletters that provide information to members of the industries about people and events, hirings and firings, acquisitions and divestitures, and changes—technological, political, and economic. For someone who wants to close deals in an industry about which he or she knows relatively little, the industry's trade journals and newsletters dating 12 months back are mandatory reading. All trade journals are listed in a directory known as *Standard Rate and Data,* and most city libraries have a copy of this book.

You can call the publishers of the respective trade journals to order back and current issues. Industry newsletters are frequently advertised in trade journals, but to make certain you haven't missed an important newsletter, you can contact The Newsletter Clearing House, Rhinebeck, New York, 914-876-2081, and ask for the names and addresses of newsletter publishers in your industry of interest.

Trade journals and newsletters must be read with the thoroughness of a detective attempting to crack a difficult mystery but without significant clues. You are specifically looking for information about the people in the organizations that you intend to sell and the factors that might influence their decisions. For instance, if the industry's most serious problem is foreign imports or the declining value of the dollar, you may want to position your premise as possibly counterbalancing that problem. If the industry's most serious financial problem is rising health-care costs, you will surely want to eliminate the addition of permanent employees on the buyer's payroll as part of your proposal. You may get lucky in your research and find profiles on your target buyer, but if not, it is time to call on the libraries.

Libraries

Once you get into the research mode, it takes on a cadence and begins to move along more quickly. Many deal people love to sell—to get in front of the buyer and wing it. But that is precisely how to lose the deal. All deals are made or broken *before* a presentation to the buyer. Dealmaking requires solid research and excellent preparation. This brings us to the Golden Rule of dealmaking:

> Ninety-five percent of the success in closing deals is the result of solid preparation before the deal meeting takes place.

Trade journals, newsletters, prospectuses, and D&B reports are good for background information, but to learn how a target buyer thinks, you will need to visit libraries. Look for the following data:

1. Newspaper articles about the company, particularly articles from the company's local newspaper.
2. Newspaper articles that quote the company's lenders.
3. Biographical information about the company's senior officers and directors.
4. A list of the company's outside directors complete with a list of their affiliations and other directorships.

Major city libraries may have some of this information on microfilm, but if you live in a city other than that of the target buyer, you will have to order it from the local newspaper in the buyer's city, or plan to visit it. Your library doubtless will have a copy of *Who's Who in Commerce and Industry*, and much of the biographical information you require will be in this thick book. It is reliable information as well, because the people in *Who's Who* provide the data themselves and have paid a fee to be included.

For independent movie producers, the most thorough directory is the *Motion Picture Almanac*. If you intend to present a deal to association managers, there is the invaluable *Encyclopedia of Associations*. The list of useful directories goes on and on, but public libraries are not able to purchase all of them.

Library Services

Fortunately, the need for research was spotted by an entrepreneurial team several years ago when they were employees in the library of McKinsey & Company, a leading management consulting firm. In that capacity, "We needed to make the McKinsey consultants well versed about industries and companies in those industries within 24 hours," said Kathleen Bingham, one of the founders of FIND/SVP, Inc., New York, one of the nation's leading library service companies. Ms. Bingham left McKinsey with Andrew Garvin, the cofounder of FIND/SVP, and they began serving clients other than McKinsey with the claim that they could answer most questions within 24 hours. Many authors, including myself, have subscribed to FIND/SVP to collect data on topics of interest. For a fee ranging from about $500 to $750, the firm will gather most of the relevant information you need to answer the question: "How will my target buyer think about and react to [my deal]?"

Library service companies such as FIND/SVP serve you best when you are able to tell them your specific need.

Interviews with Trade Journal Reporters

Another invaluable source of information on your target buyer are the reporters who cover the industry. You will get to know the names of the reporters when you read the trade journals and newsletters. They are helpful individuals particularly if the deal you are selling eventually closes and they are permitted a scoop—a story about it in advance of other publications. The law of reciprocity is alive and well among trade journalists.

You might ask the trade journal reporter if he or she knows how the leaders of the company to which you are trying to propose a deal think about the area of innovation you are proposing. You might also ask about the decision-making process at the company. And you might verify information that you learned from the CEO's secretary with the trade journal reporter.

Remember that if the trade journal reporter helps you with information, as the inimitable Mayor Richard J. Daley of Chicago used to say, "He has a clout with you." You owe him or her.

Boards of Directors

In your preparation for the deal meeting, think *associationally* as well as *linearly*. There is a tendency to think in a straight line; that is, there is my target and here am I. How do I get from here to there? Clearly, the straight line appears to be the shortest route. But associational thinking may lead to the handle that opens the door.

As you gather biographical data on the target company's senior officers and board members, particularly its outside directors, look for someone with whom you have been associated. One of the directors may have attended the university that you or someone on your team attended. Another of the directors may have worked at a firm you've worked at, or may be involved in a civic organization or charitable organization that you have devoted some time to.

If you dig deeply enough, you can find a handle that will open the door to the key decision maker, the person who can say "yes" or "no" to your deal without multiple visits. Further, if you are introduced by a company director, or a senior officer, your proposal receives a boost up the wall.

A client of my firm sought to purchase a $3 billion (total assets) financial services company. The company was publicly held, and my client did not know any of the outside board members, who appeared to be hand-picked by the CEO and were his shadows and not keen on a sale of the company in any event. The firm had an investment banker, and my client knew a senior officer at the investment banking firm; but going straight at them might have led to their finding a buyer from which they could earn an acquisition fee.

With further digging, my client found that the firm's leading salesperson was an old friend of his from Cleveland, Ohio, high school days. He called his old friend and told him that he proposed to acquire his employer and that he required an introduction to the CEO. The old school tie worked. The boyhood friend made the necessary introduction, and as these things often happen, the CEO very much wanted to sell the company but in a way that made him and the company's board of directors look good; that is, my client would have to agree to add a significant amount of capital to the company to carry out the programs that the CEO felt were important.

Perot: Master of the Close

When H. Ross Perot was an IBM computer salesperson in Dallas, he encountered a curmudgeonly CEO, the late James Ralph Wood, head of Southwestern Life Insurance Company, who did not like IBM and had no use for the computer IBM was then pushing, the IBM 7070. Southwestern did not need a computer as large as the 7070, but it was the computer that Perot was assigned to sell, and the insurance industry was the market he was assigned to sell in.

Perot learned as much as he could about Wood, that he was given to country witticisms to cut up salespeople. Perot practiced his pitch on his sales managers, and he developed responses to possible dings from Wood, such as "You're making me feel like a hunk of sausage, slicing me up a piece at a time."

Following is an excerpt from *Perot: An Unauthorized Biography* on how Perot closed the sale to Ralph Wood of Southwestern Life[*]:

> Perot enlisted IBM's president then, Gilbert E. Jones to solve his first problem—getting in to see Wood. When the IBM delegation walked in, Wood was snapping pencils in two and throwing the remnants against the wall. I hope you're not going to waste my time, Wood said, in the way of pleasantries. I could be quail hunting. Perot spoke up in the embarrassed silence. He had done his homework. He made a succinct and compelling case for harnessing a computer to Southwestern's problems. The meeting settled nothing, but Perot had his foot in the door. Wood asked his subordinate if the young guy had a life insurance background.

> Still, Perot couldn't move Wood. Southwestern Life didn't need a computer as large as the 7070. Perot proposed an offbeat solution. What if Southwestern sold unused time on its new 7070 to another company? One day, Perot stopped his partner, Campbell, and told

---

* Ibid., pp. 38–39. Reprinted here with permission.

him he was about to close the deal. How? A government agency in Dallas called the Agricultural Commodity Price Stabilization Service flew to New Orleans several times each week to use a rented 7070. Perot's plan was to secure a contract with the government agency to buy time from Southwestern Life instead and use that contract to make an irresistible offer to Ralph Wood. Campbell wondered how selling the U.S. government time on a nonexistent computer was any easier than selling anything to Ralph Wood. Not long after, Perot reported that he had closed the deal with Wood.

Perot's math won Wood over, and that was not all. Most IBM computers were leased in those days. The antitrust settlement obliged IBM to begin selling its equipment because the government considered leasing practices to be anticompetitive. At first, Wood wasn't interested in buying the 7070. Well, Perot said, how would you like to rent a machine for 10 percent less than IBM charges, with the same support, saving some $3,000 per month? Now Wood was interested.

Perot declared to Wood that he had been looking forward to early retirement from IBM. If Perot bought the computer and leased it to Wood—even at a 10 percent discount—he could make handsome profits because his overhead was so much lower than IBM's. Service-conscious IBM would take care of his machine in any event.

Where would you get $1.3 million? Wood shot back.

Mr. Wood, Perot replied, your word is good in this town. Based on our contract I could go to any bank and borrow the money. I don't think you like the idea of paying your competitors 6 percent interest, so I'm going to let you buy it instead.

Perot made the sale by thinking associationally rather than linearly. He got the appointment with Wood by having a third party make the door-opening telephone call. Once in the meeting, he was tossed out but made a good impression by showing his knowledge of the buyer. Then, at the *closing* meeting, Perot offered to broker Southwestern's unused computer time to others in need of computing power but without the funds to buy their own.

Notice also the DEP factor that Perot utilized to close the Southwestern deal. It was not Southwestern's need for an IBM 7070. Rather, it was the notion that Southwestern could make money by renting excess computer time to others.

Todd Mason points out that in playing the role "as an unpaid broker of Southwestern's second and third shifts" put him in a gray area with his employer. Granted, it was a quaint notion that customers could switch off something as expensive as a 7070 mainframe after eight hours and go home. But on the face of it, a company that bought Southwestern's second shift to satisfy its computing needs no longer was looking to buy a computer of its own. Thus, it was only a matter of time before Perot saw more opportunities for personal growth by providing services that IBM was unable to provide. Within a year of the Southwestern sale, Perot had left IBM to start Electronic Data Systems Corporation.

The error most frequently made by deal-makers is that they begin selling before they are prepared to meet with buyers. This is known as the "fire, aim, ready" school of deal-making, which works if there are an unlimited number of buyers to call on and the deal-maker has an unlimited amount of time and capital resources to keep his or her rifle loaded. Eventually, something will get hit and fall, and the deal-maker can run in its direction. But this expense in time and money can be mitigated by learning a great deal about your buyer before approaching him or her. This rule applies both to selling cereal to millions of people and to selling a million-dollar computer to a single customer.

3

How to Get Past the Gatekeepers

I am frequently asked by businessmen and women how I came up with the concept of the gatekeeper. When I lived in New York I always seemed to be stopped at a tollgate when I was in the greatest hurry to get down the road. The truth is, there are gatekeepers at the tollgates in every phase of our lives and in nearly every market in which we do business.

> For every deal, there is always a gatekeeper: someone or some group who stands in the way of the deal getting done.

How did the concept of the gatekeeper arise and how do successful deal-makers get around it?

BARRIERS THAT CAN HOLD UP DEALS

Markets are highways lined with consumers. The principal task of companies, and the reason we are in business, is to make our product or service a substitute for all other products or services while making competitive products or services no substitute for ours. The most effective means for doing this is to identify a need shared by a large number of people, then provide a solution to the problem that is highly effective and less expensive than the problem. Once this is done, the problem-solving company has created a highway to its consumers, who expect to receive a continual supply of solutions from the company. This is what entrepreneurship is all about.

But to sustain an entrepreneurial success, the problem-solving company must move quickly to erect *barriers to entry* by competitive companies. These barriers to entry I refer to as tollgates. They exist in markets, within companies, and within countries (where they are known as tariffs). If entrepreneurs don't erect them, governments will, because governments need income as much as do companies.

Figure 3.1 lists ten tollgates that all of us are familiar with.

Figure 3.1
EXAMPLES OF FAMILIAR TOLLGATES

The Product or Service	The Gatekeeper	Consumer Needs
1. Feature length films	Movie distribution companies	To see excellent movies in clean, convenient theaters at low prices
2. Effective therapies for life-threatening diseases	The U.S. Food and Drug Administration	To cure diseases that threaten their lives
3. Consumer electric products	Underwriters Laboratories	To have efficient low-priced consumer electric products
4. Beautician services	State licensing agencies	To have hair cuts, perms, and coloring in clean, convenient beauty salons and at low prices
5. Computer software products	Product reviewers for computer magazines	To have the most useful and cost-effective soft ware
6. Hovercraft services to take people from Long Island, Westchester, and Connecticut to work in New York City	The Triborough Bridge and Tunnel Authority that collects tolls on roads in New York and New Jersey	To get to work quickly, comfortably, and inexpensively

7. A consumer satellite to offer access to library material via home television	The U.S. National Aeronautics and Space Administration	To obtain answers to virtually any book 24 hours a day at a minimal cost
8. Paintings or sculptures by a new artist	Art dealers	To see new art in convenient locations
9. Inexpensive legal services	Laws in 19 states that prohibit legal advertising	To obtain inexpensive legal services
10. A safe car—one whose passengers survive a head-on crash at 55 mph	A dealership network	To drive safely without concern for one's life and the lives of family members

These examples are but a handful of the millions of gatekeepers that stand in the way of low-cost products and services and innovative products or services that obtrude in our daily lives. Prices of goods and services would be substantially lower without the existence of tollgates. Commuters could travel from Poughkeepsie to New York City in 30 minutes via hovercraft, rather than one and one half hours by train or two and one half hours by car, were it not for the gatekeepers that profit or maintain full employment at the companies that pour concrete highways or who operate the trains that go into and out of New York City carrying 6 million commuters each day.

THE TOLLGATE IN FRONT OF THE DRUG CRISIS

In one of the late John D. MacDonald's books, *The Lonely Silver Rain*, a solution to the drug crisis is suggested: The President suddenly and without notice would change the color and look of paper currency. I thought MacDonald had the nugget of a brilliant idea, and I wrote a short business plan to support it.

In my plan, the federal government would suddenly print red $100 bills, blue $50 bills, and purple $20 bills and require all citizens to go to their banks within 30 days, turn in their old bills, and receive the new, colored currency. Green paper money would become worthless immediately.

Drug dealers then would be caught between a rock and a hard place. If they showed up with tens of thousands of dollars in cash, they would be questioned as to its source. If they did not exchange their money, they would be too broke to purchase more drugs. Drug traffic would stop until new dealers took over, using the new colorful money. They would live with uncertainty as to when the money would change color again. This level of risk would drive half the drug dealers out of business. The remainder would cease activities at the next change of color.

The company that creates the colored paper money becomes a deal waiting to happen. A deal-maker could formulate the problem in depth, perhaps by interviewing officials in the Drug Enforcement Agency—particularly with regard to the flow of money—and measure the effect of the colored money exchange solution, PERT chart it, define the cost to the government, to banks, and to innocent people, and then begin an intense lobbying campaign in Washington to force the plan through channels.

The first step would be to make a product that could be attached to paper money without defacing it—say, a small tin clip like the ones museums hand out to those who enter. The clip would be stamped with a message or symbol to show that the bill to which it is attached was *not* used to pay for drugs.

The entrepreneurial company would pay for the production of millions of these clips with donations from wealthy concerned individuals and corporations. This would be *celebrity endorsement*—having a dozen or so highly respected Americans lend their names to the project.

The clips would be given to commercial and savings banks in a test community. The banks would then give the clips out to customers, retail businesses, community groups, schools, churches, and cultural institutions with the intent of having 100 percent utilization. Celebrity endorsement would assist in generating broad acceptance of the project, and the entrepreneur would glean publicity.

A newsletter as well would provide information as to how the plan is working. The entrepreneurial company could also run a currency-design contest. Dances and concerts could be sponsored, as well as parades. With the test community running smoothly, the entrepreneurial company could undertake *facilities management* contracts with other cities to introduce the same kind of credibility-building programs there. The cash flow would build significantly, enabling the company to produce prototype currency and to demonstrate to the federal government its ability to produce new currency and get it into the banking system. To make the company an ongoing proposition rather than a one-shot deal, the currency would have to be changed at random every so often until drug dealers give up their trade.

I suggested this plan to two officials of the U.S. Drug Enforcement Agency. They thought the idea was very good and suggested that I pass it along through proper channels to President Ronald Reagan. I did, and a few months later I received a thank you note from Nancy Reagan and that's as far as the proposal went.

Nonplussed, I asked a few politician friends why an idea as inexpensive and elegant as having everyone turn in their old greenbacks in exchange for new currency, thus obsoleting the cash held by drug dealers, would not be well-received by officials at the highest level of government.

"It's simple," my friends told me. "There are lots of politicians with cash in shoe boxes and safety deposit boxes who would lose money as well."

HOW TO AVOID TOLLGATES

No deal can be closed unless tollgates are circumvented. And since tollgates stand in front of every deal, learning to "shun the pike"—an old American idiom for avoiding tollgates—is essential in successful deal-making.

As the deal-maker knows, the word *no* means that negotiations have begun. The sale begins with the "no," the great ones will tell you. Some deal-makers respond by buying the tollgate. Others, for whom owning the tollgate is not core to their business, implement negotiating skills and circumvent it. Still others who find the tollgate too expensive circumvent the tollgate by forming cooperative alliances with clout.

Finding a way to get around tollgates is a great American tradition. Deal-makers have so thoroughly refined it that it has become intrinsic to their management approach.

Hunter-collectors of prehistoric tribal communities devised their own selective leveraging techniques to gain access to the most important highway in their economic system: the chief. Bronislaw Malinowski and other anthropologists have written that the chief would not even face the hunter-collectors, much less speak to them, unless they returned from the hunts with very large gifts—massive lion skins or enormous elephant tusks—so big that new community centers had to be erected to house them. After the hunter-collector built the large community center, he customarily provided a feast with dancing, celebration and beautiful costumes. Only then would the chief turn to the hunter-collector and invite him to sit next to him.

Corporate raiders are today's hunter-collectors. After they have made a few hundred million dollars, they seek access to the chiefs of society. They give wings to museums, buildings to universities, and operating rooms to hospitals. They throw parties and hold feasts, and their friends buy new ball gowns and tuxedos. The events are captured by the society pages. Some chiefs of society attend the hunter-collectors' parties and permit the deal-makers to drink and eat with them. Other chiefs say, "You have not paid a large enough toll." And the deal-makers return to their marketplace, take over another large company, extract their cash, and renegotiate with the chiefs. This time they offer to build a new museum for the community and endow a new art collection (a shun-the-pike offer) or give the same amount to the old museum (a large toll). The chiefs think about the offer and agree that the hunter-collector may join their board of directors (be admitted to their highway) in return for the gift.

Shunning the pike is a primitive custom. Elegant deal-making restates it as a system.

LEARNING TO SPOT THE INSIDE GATEKEEPERS

If you look at marketplaces as consumers alongside highways and highways as having no tolls (the ones that cash-poor entrepreneurs use), medium-price tolls (where the consumers are cash-poor but can be persuaded to buy if they are pummeled with advertising), and high-price tolls (where the consumers are cash-rich and interested in new products), then you can design a strategy to buy the pike, shun the pike, build a new pike, or (the cop-out route) lobby the government to operate the pike.

Your company's union is a strong cooperative alliance-style pike. Your boss may be like the Dutchman or prehistoric chief-style pike operator. Your company's data processing department may be a time-constrained pike, the manager protesting continually that he or she "cannot get to" your job for at least a week. Your company's accounting and finance department may be an overworried pike, its people unable to find the cash to pay for senior management's wish list.

Tollgates often spring up when brash, bright M.B.A.s join tradition-bound companies. M.B.A.'s annoy people with their appearance, education, and manner of speaking. The chiefs of the many different departments, even the chief switchboard operator, turn their backs on them. M.B.A.s must frequently learn to unbutton their button-down styles and snip the tassels off their loafers before the chiefs will permit them access to the information they have to have to do their jobs.

Fellow employers often do not communicate the price of the toll at their pike. Speaking about tollgate prices is not an accepted practice in the society that operates within a company. You have never heard the chief supervisor say to the new M.B.A. who is examining the possibility of changing the conveyor lines to enable more workers to catch defects, "Come right in, young woman, and let's see what you have in mind. By the way, I will not cooperate unless you share the credit for your improvements with me and, of course, convince me that they will save the company money. But I will cooperate with you if you give me part of the credit. That's my price."

Fellow workers are *nonverbal communicators*. You have to spot the inside gatekeepers to see the message that they communicate.

TIPS ON GAINING A GATEKEEPER'S COOPERATION

The coworker's gut values are his or her tollgate. These values can block an innovative plan as thoroughly and completely as the FDA can stop an innovative drug from coming onto the market. But the deal-maker can gain the *cooperation* of the blocking coworker by understanding his or her gut values and communicating emphatically. Let's begin with the basics.

Controlling the Conversation with Questions

Somers H. White, a communications consultant and uniquely gifted speaker and trainer of speakers, explains the methodology of convincing people to do things for you that they had no intention of doing. White asks to borrow a pen. The willing victim hands White a pen. He says thank you, then breaks it in half and throws the pieces away.

Before the person can speak, White hands him or her a pencil and says, "Here's a ten-cent pencil to replace your eighty-nine cent pen. Are we even?" he asks.

The willing victim replies no.

White continues, "But have you thought about how much more useful a pencil is than a pen? Why, a pencil can do many more things than a pen. I bet you can name fifteen things that you can do with a pencil that you can't do with a pen." The willing victim thinks a second. He or she begins naming the things—erase, write upside down, shade—and then gets into the game with gusto. By the time the victim crosses ten on the way to fifteen, he or she has forgotten that the smiling questioner broke the pen.

If you can control the meeting with questions, White says, you can convince people to do things for you. In order to convince a plant manager in your company to switch from employee time cards and manual inventory controls to computer-based job tracking, for instance, requires that the deal-maker ask questions continually. For example, he or she should find out who is involved in tracking production costs, the years they have been doing it, the benefits of the system, the possibility of retraining them for other tasks, their degree of loyalty to the plant manager, and their importance to the manager's power base. This gives the deal-maker a feeling for the level of the plant manager's technical sophistication and what he or she has at stake if the personnel and inventory controls are automated.

The deal-maker should insert questions throughout the interview, on the order of:

How many times a day does raw material arrive at the plant?

Do you think we could change this to fewer deliveries?

What is your experience in speaking with our suppliers?

Do you think we could switch to just-in-time deliveries?

When gatekeepers are asked questions by deal-makers who are effective communicators they are drawn into the deal-maker's world and begin to identify more closely with the deal. Persuasion is not a hard sell; it is asking questions, learning about the gatekeeper, and then involving him or her in the inside plan.

Understanding the Other Person's Gut Values

When the deal-maker first sees the "buyer," the first things he or she notices are his or her sex and age. Assume, for example, that the deal-maker is a thirty-seven-year-old male and the gatekeeper is a sixty-three-year-old male. As the deal-maker enters the buyer's room, he logs in the following data: Male, born about 1930, raised in the Depression, probably served in Korea, delayed in getting a degree, probably did not get into the job market until his mid-twenties. The deal-maker sizes the gatekeeper up as born and raised poor and unwilling to take chances with an overweening, spoon-fed, pampered, thirty-seven-year old corporate hotshot.

Early in the conversation the thirty-seven year old must find an opening to let the sixty-three year old know that his suffering and personal drive to overcome depression roots and a GI bill college degree have not gone unnoticed. The thirty-seven year old can blow it by coming across as a "wise ass," or he can do it just right and gain a supporter.

Nothing obvious like "Tell me what was it really like growing up during the Depression." But maybe something like "You remind me a little of [a thirties or forties man-of-the-people hero like Gene Sarazen or Red Grange]." If he thinks the deal-maker is sincere, the buyer will leap at the opportunity to talk about himself. The buyer will say a number of things about his origins or family or background that will provide hooks to hang on to later in the conversation. The important things for the deal-maker to listen for are gut values.

It is likely that the sixty-three-year-old buyer has positive feelings for things traditional, for convention; he is cautious, likes stability, doesn't like upset. The deal-maker could adjust his presentation to be responsive to those values. He could say something like "We've developed a cautious attitude at the senior level," "We want to avoid risk and uncertainty in our manufacturing operations; quality control procedures are out of an old engineering textbook," and so forth.

With a younger buyer, perhaps one in his mid-fifties, the gut values were formed in the early 1950s, but he or she will have to be drawn out more to determine whether he or she was early fifties—Doris Day and Guy Mitchell—or rock 'n' roll and Elvis. In any event, it is critical to take an accurate reading of the buyer's gut values before proceeding with the presentation. All could be lost by using a painful word or phrase when a friendlier one could work miracles.

Giving Inside Information

Once you have established that you are a good listener and you are sensitive to the people in the trenches, it is the time to take the gatekeeper into your confidence, share your plans, and persuade him or her to raise the gate and permit innovation to occur in his or her domain. The plant manager wants inside information, a view of the big picture, and, if he or she buys the plan, credit for turning the pike.

The deal-maker begins by explaining to the gatekeeper that the company is on a "slash expenses and raise cash" path. It intends to improve its cash flow in every conceivable manner and to thereby raise cash to make acquisitions, enter new markets, introduce new products, repurchase stock, take the company private, or whatever the goal may be. Key personnel such as the plant manager will be compensated based on the cash flow of their divisions. This means that the gatekeeper will receive bonuses based on how much cash his or her division puts into the shoebox each month.

"Why do you want to change things? Haven't I run a profitable division for over fifteen years?" the plant manager asks.

"Yes, you have," the deal-maker responds. "But our company is a sitting duck for a raid, and we have three choices: lead, follow, or get out of the way. Senior management has decided to lead in order to protect what you and others have built over the years. This means service to our customers, loyalty to our employees, and increased value to our stockholders."

"Nice speech, but you know you mean layoffs and squeezing the workers for their last drop of blood," replies the plant manager.

"All right, too much soapbox, I admit," responds the deal-maker. "But we think—and we would like to share your ideas on the subject—that we can manage this company more efficiently and more profitably than any takeover fund or corporate raider."

"I'm not buying your story," responds the plant manager. "What could we do to run this plant more efficiently and more profitably?"

With that, you can begin to pull out your plans, comparative cost analyses, and proposed production changes. This is your chance to gain an ally by giving him inside information.

But this objective will be lost if the deal-maker does not understand the gut values of the plant manager and affects a pretentious, know-it-all posture.

Perhaps the leading student of the personality characteristics of corporate managers, Michael Maccoby (*The Gamesman,* New York: Simon & Schuster, 1975), interviewed 250 corporate executives and asked them to list the character traits "important for your work" and those that were "stimulated or reinforced by your work." Seventy-four percent of the managers said that cooperativeness was important to their work, but only 37 percent said that cooperativeness was stimulated by their work. If one is to win the trust and cooperation of the plant managers and division heads, they must be provided a bigger picture and made to feel part of the deal-maker's world.

Use Information Skillfully

The key to getting around the tollgate and getting the meeting is the skillful use of information. Either you have an overwhelming need to gain information from the buyer, or, conversely, you have special information to impart to him or her, data not contained in the plan that you submitted and that the buyer will be excited to learn about.

This is known as the information solution: It is the key that raises the tollgate and allows you access to the decision maker. It may not close the deal, but at this stage of the game nobody has turned past the first page of your proposal anyhow so a closing is the remotest of dreams.

The alternative tactic is to give information: the elegant bluff approach. This is the poker analogy described in Chapter 6, where you withhold information in order to appear simple and bluffable. Here's how it works when you're trying to get a meeting with a buyer.

Telephone (or FAX) the buyer and if you cannot be put through, tell the secretary to please clip the following note to the deal that was recently sent in. Describe the color of the notebook or other features and repeat the name of the deal.

"Now, here's the note to clip onto the cover," you say.

> The negotiations with (so-and-so well-known major player) mentioned on page 3 of the proposal have resulted in a contract for X-million.

Ask the secretary to read it back to you. Then offer your thanks.

By understating in the typed proposal, you have the right, indeed you are expected, to clarify and bring the proposal up-to-date. Moreover, the plan with the note clipped to it will be put on the top of the stack of incoming deals on the buyer's desk.

The Moving Train Effect—Convince the Buyer to Act Quickly

To persuade the gatekeeper to act quickly it is important that the deal-maker create the impression that the train (that is, the deal) is leaving the station and those passengers who are not on board will be left behind. If a deal sits on the buyer's desk or in-box for too long, the cadence is broken and the deal falls apart.

To create a sense of movement around your deal, continually add updates to the business plan via telephone, FAX, and mail. Think of them as bright little stocking stuffers that are attached to the main package to keep it near the top of the in-box stack. The updates must relay important information that amplifies the data in the package itself.

Some examples are the following:

> Jane Smith, who is one of the top salespeople in our industry, has agreed to leave her position at Jones Engineering where she has been earning over $125,000 per year to join us as Vice President—Sales for less remuneration, but an equity position.

> I thought you would like to know that orders for the previous month were $300,000 above the dollar amount projected in the business plan, and profits were $50,000 greater for the same period.

> Just a brief note to let you know that Charles Smith, the recently retired CEO of Ahab Fishing Vessels, Inc., has joined our board of directors and invested $20,000 in common stock. We are pleased to have him involved. His investment is very timely, and we will be able to ship more product this month than last, thus enabling us to break into the black sooner than expected.

A continuous flow of these letters, sprinkled with telephone calls and the occasional FAX message gives your deal a sense of movement and direction. It is chugging down the track, while the other deals in the in-box just sit there without motion or rhythm.

4

NETWORKING AND GIVING CREDIT: SELECTIVE LEVERAGE TECHNIQUES

By spreading credit for your deal among many players you bring together the energy and contacts of people who stand to win if the deal closes and to lose if it craters. This is known as networking the deal or leveraging the players.

AIR SPACE MARKETING

Supermarket or other retail store managers can be leveraged selectively if you offer them a profitable product that they can sell in *air space*, space that they are not presently using for products and that does not require a capital expenditure. Note the plethora of products that hang on J-hooks near the checkout counters of Wal-Mart and K-Mart stores. Gossip magazines are placed on racks near checkout counters. The *National Enquirer* sells 3,000,000 copies per year in air space.

Assume that you have developed a consumer product that can be sold at retail for less than $5 per unit and that earns a profit of 50 percent for the retailer. To attempt to gain shelf facings for a new and untested product is virtually impossible. Supermarket chains and certain other retailers have begun to charge "slotting fees" to consumer goods producers who wish to test new products and line extensions. The real estate inside retail stores has become very dear. To avoid slotting fees, consumer goods producers are offering to place their goods at the ends of aisles, on racks near the checkout counter, on the checkout counters themselves, or jutting out of aisles on coat-hanger-sized hooks.

One innovative food producing company that has shunned the slotting fee tollgate is Oven Poppers, Inc., Manchester, New Hampshire, founded and managed by Stacy Kimball. Ms. Kimball and her partner have developed a line of fresh-frozen seafood dinners and have called on most of the supermarket chains in New England to put the products on their shelves. As if they were all singing out of the same choir book, each supermarket manager said that they would be pleased to put Oven Poppers on their shelves for a fee. And they weren't talking clam chowder. "One of the larger chains asked us to pay a slotting allowance of $20,000 per month," Ms. Kimball told me.

To circumnavigate this problem, Ms. Kimball developed a selective leveraging strategy. She developed an attractive, brightly-colored, traffic-stopping, end-of-the-aisle, bucketlike container. Into the container she placed her seafood boxes in a cluttered manner. Ms. Kimball traipsed back to the supermarkets after scheduling appointments with the managers and displayed the containers at the end of aisles that did not have gross-margin-producing items; rather, they had discount items such as off-brand beverages.

Then, to make the managers an offer they could not refuse, Ms. Kimball promised to generate new customers for the stores via an intensive, all-out public relations campaign geared to the media in their markets. If the seafood did not sell, the managers were under no obligation to reorder. But, Oven Poppers would not pay slotting fees.

Ms. Kimball won the gamble. The newspapers created *demand pull through* for the products, and Ms. Kimball received sufficient reorders to launch her fledgling company. The key to her close was the implicit guarantee that the stores' air space at the ends of aisles would generate a drove of new customers at high gross profit margins.

If the store managers were unhappy with the results, they had no obligation to Ms. Kimball. The managers got the credit for stocking innovative, healthy products. They got the credit for increasing sales. And they got the credit for higher profits. The deals closed.

SELECTIVELY LEVERAGING
THE IRS AUDITOR

Nothing more frightens a typical American taxpayer than being notified of an IRS audit. People react to an audit with a range of emotions along the fear curve, from "My God! I'll be sent to Leavenworth," to "I don't have any time to go through an audit." Neither of these extremes, nor any of the degrees of fear along the spectrum, are helpful.

The government is a business—a very large business—operated by people who, for the most part, have never been in business. They do not plan, think, or implement their plans as you or I do in our businesses. For instance, if the government collected all of its accounts receivable—that is, its taxes—it would not have to implement new taxes. Regrettably, that will never happen because political power is in essence the ability to levy or lift taxes.

Whereas our business credo is get the *cash before you crash,* the government's credo appears to be complicate, obfuscate, then confiscate. Once you understand the government's premise in auditing taxpayers (rather than collecting from tax avoiders and loophole users), you are in a position to win the audit game.

The second step in problem-formulating for your tax audit is to understand that the auditor does not know very much. I am sure you have seen the newspaper articles where a reporter asks a question concerning the proper entries in an income tax return of six different IRS officials and receives six different answers. IRS auditors go to school upon being hired for their jobs, but the rules and regulations are much too complicated, and frequently subject to interpretation, for them to understand in all cases what is and what is not a proper entry or deduction. They know one thing, however. You probably owe them money and they are going to get it.

Step three in winning the audit game is not to go into it alone. Take with you the most experienced certified public accountant you can find; especially one who has experienced many IRS audits. One who attends seminars on interpreting the tax codes. One who is familiar with all regulations, or if not, knows where to go for answers. CPAs such as this have no fear of tax audits: They enjoy them as much as a child loves an ice cream cone at a Fourth of July parade.

I have observed a skilled CPA selectively leveraging an IRS auditor. She gives him one or two small victories in the $100 to $300 range. She explains complicated areas of the tax code to him, so that he will not embarrass himself in the future. Then she finds areas of either overpaid or underdeducted expenses and very gently says, "Well, I suppose we will have to file an amended return to get some of the client's money back."

If you are going through a tax audit now, put the brakes on and find the right CPA immediately. Do not fight with the auditor. Do not stick your feet in the sand. The auditor will turn the matter over to the *collection* department and that will be a pit stop in hell. If you have never been audited, you probably will be at some time in the future. So, here are some tips:

1. Do not try to maximize your deductions on your tax returns. Leave a little on the table so that in the event of an audit you will have some wins on your side of the table from the beginning.

2. The Travel and Entertainment deduction is the area of an income tax return where auditors expect to score their biggest victories. Do not take deductions in this area that are unsupportable and undocumentable. You will lose all of them.

3. Remember that you cannot be audited every year. Once you have been audited for a specific year, the IRS cannot audit you for another two years.

The key to selectively leveraging an IRS auditor is to hire a skilled CPA who understands the tax code better than does the auditor and who can give the auditor more than money to take back with him or her. Information and understanding will help the auditor move up the chain of command more than a big score in an audit will.

MOVIE FINANCING:
HOW TO RAISE MONEY UPFRONT

An independent movie producer reads a script just presented to him by a writer. He likes it and signs an option to pay the writer $75,000 plus 5 percent of the producer's gross income.* Very highly regarded writers receive 10 times this amount upfront. The producer must pay the writer $25,000 within 90 days and $50,000 by the first day of shooting.

The producer thinks that a marginally well-known actor who costarred in a recent successful film would be a good male lead, and he is considered affordable, bondable, and bankable. These are important characteristics. Some stars such as Dustin Hoffman or Jack Nicholson are simply not affordable by most independent producers. They want several million dollars plus a large percentage of the distributors' gross income, sometimes as much as $5 million plus 10 percent. Bondable means that the actor or director has a reputation for hard, focused work in order to bring the film in on budget. Some stars have been known to come to the set unprepared to work, thus blowing a day of shooting at great cost to the producer. Performance bonds are not obtainable on these people. Without bonds, the producer cannot convince lenders that the budget is realistic. If financing cannot be arranged for overruns, the film cannot be finished; thus no revenue stream.

Bankable means that the revenue projections are believable. If an actor's last few movies had box office results of $10 million, $8 million, and $6 million in that order, then projecting that his next film will do $15 million will convince no one. If his last film achieved box office results of $30 million, projecting $20 million for the current project is more likely.

---

* Producer's gross income means income after the exhibitors' or box office's receipts—generally 50 percent of the ticket price.

The producer calls the actor's agent to ask that he read the script. This process is done rapidly, and, if all goes well, the actor agrees to take the role. The producer and the agent negotiate a flat $250,000 price for the actor's services, payable $25,000 on signing, $112,500 on the first day of shooting, and $112,500 on the last day of shooting. This is a rather modest contract and fee. Certain stars demand much more upfront money and other privileges, such as the right to change the script, approve the director, receive a percentage of the producer's gross income, and select where their name will appear in the advertisements. Whenever you see a strange grouping of names of relatively equally ranked actors, such as Michael Caine, Sean Connery, and George C. Scott, you can be sure that each wanted to appear to the left of the other two and not on a line below. The compromise is sometimes a pyramid, or a pyramid of their faces and names on a straight line. The negotiations are so tedious and difficult that movie producers sometimes survive on antacid liquids and tension relievers.

The independent producer now has a script and a star. He needs a director. The best directors are usually booked well into the future, so it is up to the producer to find out who is available, what his or her track record is, and what he or she will cost. With three less well-known players—producer, writer and male lead—a "name" director is called for. For this, he flies to Los Angeles and begins searching for the optimum candidate.

Finally, a top director is found and agrees to $400,000 for 16 weeks of shooting, 8 weeks before, and 16 weeks of editing, plus 5 percent of the distributors' gross. He or she receives $80,000 on signing, $120,000 on the first day of shooting, and $200,000 on the final day of shooting, to be protected by a letter of credit. In consideration for the $80,000 advance payment, the director agrees to deliver a budget and an edited shooting script to the producer within 60 days from the date of signing the contract and receiving his or her first installment.

To summarize what has happened to this point, an independent producer has obtained the rights to a script and the services of an actor and a director for a certain period of time. Nothing has been paid for; everything is still a projection. However, the producer does have commitments from three professionals, and he has forward movement on his side.

The independent producer has to move quickly to convert the commitments to firm obligations, and that takes cash. Here are his needs:

Writer: $25,000 in 60 days (30 days of the 90–day deadline have passed); plus $50,000 on the first day of shooting, say, 120 days from now.

Male Lead: $25,000 within 60 days, plus $112,500 on the first day of shooting and $112,500 on the final day of shooting.

Director: $80,000 within 60 days, plus $120,000 on the first day of shooting, plus $200,000 on the final day of shooting.

The cost of the film, its budget, will be prepared by the director, in conjunction with the writer, upon his receipt of $80,000. Thus, the immediate need is for $130,000 plus $20,000 for expenses. And, he must deliver a letter of credit for $320,000 to guarantee the director payment in full. How is this raised? Essentially, by leveraging the *endorsements* of the three committed players, particularly that of the director.

The second payment date is on the first day of shooting, approximately 120 days from now, requiring $282,500. As it would be foolish to raise the initial $150,000 plus the letter of credit without knowing that the $282,500 was committed for, the producer's near-term goal is to close on $432,500, plus the letter of credit for $320,000.

To raise his upfront capital, the independent producer "sells" the least valuable rights to the movie. To a nonmovie entrepreneur, this is the same as leveraging off-balance sheet assets.

The independent producer has several off-balance sheet assets he can sell. These are as follows:

1. *U.S. Theatrical Distribution:* The right to distribute the film to U.S. theaters for a fee equal to from 25 percent to 60 percent of distributors' gross income, a U.S. distributor such as 20th

Century Fox or MGM might advance all or a portion of its budget. The more the corporations advance, the greater their percentage ownership of the film. Independent producers would rather negotiate with more tender lambs for the money than enter the jaws of the U.S. distributor. For an unknown producer, trying to get upfront money is about as easy as getting a stubborn hound dog from under a porch in 110 degree weather. But dealing with them at some point is inevitable.

2. *Foreign Theatrical Distributors:* The rights to distribute the film in 30 to 50 foreign countries are quite easily sold at the film industry's annual trade show: the Cannes Film Festival. A French distributor advanced Francis Coppolla $100,000 for the French rights to *Apocalypse Now* in the bar of the Carlyle Hotel in Cannes in May 1979; and when the film was number one at the box office for most of 1980, the French distributor made over 20 times its investment.

3. *U.S. Network Television:* The three major U.S. television networks are forever in the market for product. They buy movies by the pound; that is, four hours are worth twice as much as two hours. They agree not to broadcast the film for several years. The one hour of out-takes to King Kong were put back into the two-hour film for the television sale, which brought the price up by $2.5 million to $7.5 million. The film Annie was sold to a network for $20 million to finance the shooting. It was not a good investment.

4. *U.S. Independent Television:* After a couple of runs on one of the networks, the independent stations would like to fill some of their hours of programming time with Hollywood's finest. Because the air time will be in the future, the advance from the independents is less than from the networks; but, the product is nonetheless salable to them.

5. *U.S. Cable Television:* An increasingly important market for Hollywood's product is cable television. It has the audience, hence the capital to pay a fair penny for its chance to show any film. Forty-seven million homes are wired for cable TV in the United States; the only major city without cable television

is Chicago. A subset of this market is pay television, but it is not in every market as yet and represents a smaller source of cash.

6. *Home Video:* With the explosive sales of VCRs, the market for watching movies at home is estimated currently at 110 percent of theatrical. If a film grosses $20 million at U.S. box offices, it should generate $22 million in home videocassette rentals over the subsequent three to five years. Thus, the home video rights to a film can be sold for a significant amount.

7. *In-Flight:* This is a small but interesting market in which to sell rights. For in-flight, the film must be rated G or PG and must be not more than 90 minutes in length.

8. *Book Rights:* Is there a paperback book possibility in this script?

9. *Product Rights:* In the film *Rocky III*, when Rocky smiles at his little boy and says "Wheaties! What are Wheaties?" and the child giggles uncontrollably and says to Rocky, "The breakfast of champions," I could see the check from General Mills to the *Rocky III* producers. My estimate: $300,000.

10. *Leverageable Assets:* If you are a George Lucas, capable of conceiving of the "Federation" and producing movies that depict wars between the stars, then you might end up with toys, games, calendars, clothing, bed linen, and robots as well. LucasFilms could be one of the *Fortune* 500 largest industrial companies on its product sales alone. The $40 Darth Vadar mask sold close to 25,000 copies.

Who and What Is Being Leveraged?

As one of the first corporate raiders, Meshulam Riklis, who built an empire between 1950 and 1970 of companies with combined revenues of $2 billion on an initial stake of $25,000, was fond of saying, "Success in business is the effective nonuse of cash." In the case of a first-time producer raising $800,000 to close a writer, a star, and a director, the effective nonuse of cash traces the following pattern:

1. Find an excellent script.
2. Attract an affordable lead actor who needs and likes the script.
3. Leverage the script and star to bait, hook, and land a big director.
4. Pause: Note either the actor or the director, or both, must be bankable; that is, you can take their track records to the bank; they are collateral.
5. Raise the money to secure the services of the writer, star, and director by leveraging their names and track records with a source (or sources) of cash that want(s) a right(s) to release the movie.

Of the ten off balance sheet assets or sources of cash flow, the two that you least want to lose upfront are U.S. theatrical and U.S. home video. In Figure 4.1, you can see the scope and breadth of these two enormous markets and why you want to hold on to them:

Figure 4.1
SHARES OF DOMESTIC MOVIE REVENUES (a)

	1984		1989	
Category	$Millions	%	$Millions	%
Box Office Receipts	$4,030	49.0%	$ 5,022	30.0
Television	2,385	29.0	4,018	24.0
Broadcast TV	905	11.0	1,506	9.0
Pay Cable TV	1,480	18.0	2,511	15.0
Video Cassettes	1,810	22.0	7,700	46.0
	$8,225	100.0%	$16,740	100.0%

(a) Source: Veronis, Suhler & Associates Communications Industry Forecast, 1990, New York, pp. 82–83. Reprinted here with permission.

If the independent movie producer can raise enough upfront money by selling the pay/cable rights or the television broadcast rights, he or she has applied *selective leverage* in a nonmajor cash flow channel. What is significant here is that a peripheral asset is leveraged to raise money for the core.

> To raise the upfront money for a deal, always apply selective leverage: Borrow on a peripheral asset and protect the core business.

The independent film producer could have sold the foreign rights just as easily, but this would depend on whether or not the story line is of interest to a nondomestic audience. Certain subjects, such as fantasy, gangster, shoot-'em-ups and America-bashing, do very well in many foreign markets. Adventure films and romantic comedies do not do as well.

The Next Step

Once the director is "bought and paid for," he or she prepares a shooting script and budgets it to the penny. A producer's fee of $250,000, plus or minus, is part of the budget, of course. A bankable director always brings his or her movies in on budget; hence, you can "take them to the bank." The producer can visit the Entertainment Industry Loan Department of a commercial bank or asset-based lender and borrow a significant percentage of the budget from the lender by pledging one or more of the existing assets. The collateral is released when the film is "in the can"; that is, has been shot, edited, cut, and ready for distribution and sale.

Alternatively, the producer can finance the budget by visiting a distributor—Paramount, Universal, Orion, Twentieth Century Fox—or a cable company such as HBO or Showtime, and trade the rights to that market for money. These financiers act as venture capital funds and extract a piece of the action for their money. The earlier in the project that they are called upon, the larger the cut. If the producer holds off, he or she can go to them with a movie in the can and ask them to finance the print and advertising budget, which is frequently smaller than the shooting budget, and give up perhaps 35 percent of the revenues for that particular channel.

With only three or four assets leveraged selectively , the producer can hold onto the other rights in their entirety as well as a large percentage of the cash flow from the core assets. If the movie does well, a great reputation plus multiple channels is earned. If the movie does not do well, the producer has earned $250,000 and he or she is off the first rung of the ladder. A resumé is begun.

Uncomplicating the Deal

You will notice when observing the business landscape over an extended period of time that all industries become simplified over time. That is because there is a significant profit to be made by making products and services faster, less expensive, and more efficient. Computers, when first introduced in 1968, were so large that a person could walk through them. Today, computers with more memory than the 1960s version can fit into the palm of your hand. They cost less than 1 percent of the original version as well.

Other examples abound in medical instruments, trucks, tractors, record players, swimsuits, kitchen appliances, optical lenses, writing instruments, and more. It is in the nature of competition in any free market—unaided by subsidies or tax benefits—that innovation arises by uncomplicating existing products and services. The opposite occurs, of course, in business aided by legislation and tax benefits, such as real estate development, where large is better because it produces larger tax subsidies. The *ripple effect* means that more land is condemned for development, more forests are cleared, and more population is shifted to new malls, industrial parks, and housing developments with resultant decay in inner cities, requirements for multiple beltways and dozens of spaghetti-like off-ramps, and more government employees to oversee the mess, with resultant higher taxes.

Uncomplicating the deal in the movie industry is a few short years away. With the advent of High Definition Television film (HDTV), or movies on a computer chip, if you prefer, it will soon be possible for a consumer, sitting in his or her den or at a club or deli or wherever an HDTV screen is set up, to select a movie beamed up to a satellite and down to the HDTV receiver.

When this occurs, the theatrical distributor, currently the entertainment industry's most powerful tollgate, will have to lead, follow, or get out of the way. Because the consumer will be king, and whenever this occurs in an industry the consumer can be leveraged. What does this mean exactly? It means asking the consumer to pay upfront for a product or service to be delivered later.

LEVERAGING THE CUSTOMER TO FUND YOUR DEAL

The insurance industry invented it: pay now, receive benefits later (if needed); the newspaper industry copied it; and the membership discount stores have taken it to a new high in deal-making. Leveraging the customer to fund a deal is one of the most popular ways of closing the deal to start a new business.

Leveraging the customer goes by a lot of different names, but all of the methods are based on trust. The names are *franchising, direct response marketing, gift-of-the-month club, subscription, membership, mutual funds, dealership, distributorship,* and a handful of others. Jim Bakker sold eternal salvation on a "prepaid membership" basis. Oh, how Americans love to join things!

In *Democracy in America,* written by the French political scientist Alexis de Tocqueville following a nine-month visit to America in 1831–32, we find these observations.[*]

America is a nation of joiners.

The inhabitant of the United States learns from birth that he must rely on himself to combat the ills and trials of life; he is restless and defiant in his outlook toward the authority of society and appeals to its power only when he cannot do without it. The beginnings of this attitude first appear at school, where the children, even in their games, submit to rules settled by themselves and punish offenses which they have defined themselves. The same attitude turns up again in all the affairs of social life. If some obstacle blocks the public road halting the circulation of traffic, the neighbors at once

---

[*] Alexis de Tocqueville, *Democracy in America,* Harper & Row, New York, 1969, pp.189–190.

form a deliberative body; this improvised assembly produces an executive authority which remedies the trouble before anyone has thought of the possibility of some previously constituted authority beyond that of those concerned. Where enjoyment is concerned, people associate to make festivities grander and more orderly. Finally, associations are formed to combat exclusively moral troubles: intemperance is fought in common. Public security, trade and industry, and morals and religion all provide the aims for associations in the United States. There is no end which the human is capable of attaining by the free action of the collective power of individuals.

The right of association being recognized, citizens can use its different ways. An association simply consists in the public as a formal support of specific doctrines by a certain number of individuals who have undertaken to cooperate in a stated way in order to make these doctrines prevail. Thus the right of association can almost be identified with freedom to write, but already associations are more powerful than the press. When some view a candidacy, represented by an association, it must take clearer and more precise shapes. It counts its supporters and involves them in its cause; these supporters get to know one another, and numbers increase zeal. An association unites the energies of divergent minds and vigorously directs them toward a clearly indicated goal.

Let's Make a Deal

From the founding of the country to the present, Americans have played "Let's Make A Deal." We join lodges, churches, teams, clubs, fraternal societies, boards, committees, and therapy groups. Sophisticated advertisers know that belonging is one of our great needs.

American Express tells us, "Membership has its privileges." AT&T encourages us to "Reach Out and Touch Someone." PepsiCola applauds "The Pepsi Generation." The airlines offer membership clubs at busy airports and frequent flyer programs. Some bookstore chains have copied this program, and supermarket chains are experimenting with the concept. Some consumer products companies put the word "Club" in their corporate title, such as *Diners Club, The Price Club, Book-of-the-Month Club* and *Club Mediterraine*.

All these companies were launched on the simplest of concepts: Let's Make A Deal. Pay me in advance and I will deliver a product or service or exclusive territory for the privilege of selling my product in the future. Over 80 percent of the most successful entrepreneurial companies in the country have been launched by leveraging the customer. These include:

Mary Kay Cosmetics, Inc.
  Mary Kay Ash, founder

H&R Block, Inc.
  Henry W. and
  Rich A. Bloch, founders

Carlson Companies, Inc.
    (Gold Bond trading stamps)
  Curtis L. Carlson, founder

Pizza Hut, Inc.
  Frank L. Carney, founder

Days Inn of America, Inc.
  Cecil B. Day, founder

Honda Motor Company, Ltd.
  Soichiro Honda, founder

Horchow Collection
  Roger Horchow, founder

McDonald's Corporation
  Raymond A. Kroc, founder

International Data Group, Inc.
  (ComputerWorld and other magazines)
  Patrick J. McGovern, founder

Electronic Data System Corp.
  H. Ross Perot, founder

General Nutrition, Inc.
  David B. Shakanian, founder

The U-Haul System
  Leonard S. Schoen, founder

Tandy Corporation
  Charles Tandy, founder

Holiday Inns of America, Inc.
C. Kemmons Wilson, founder

Let's explore the basic concept of leveraging the customer.

Direct Mail Markets

The simplest and in many ways the most elegant form of deal-making is essentially risk free and relies primarily on customer money, rather than on investor money. The entrepreneur can launch a direct mail company without quitting his or her job and with only a modest amount of cash up front. You can become a direct mail entrepreneur and then springboard the asset values that you create (mailing list, name recognition, supplier relationships) into other solution delivery methods, using the cash flow from the direct mail business and the market awareness that you have developed as the catalyst.

Direct mail is the process of mailing a solution to a group of people who have a problem, such that the value of the solution is perceived by the customers as greater than the cost of the problem. Direct mail is not direct response. The latter is the process of buying advertisements in print, audio, or video media to describe a solution to the problems of the general public, who, if it perceives value in the advertisement, will order the product or service by telephone or mail. Unlike direct mail, direct response requires a considerable amount of cash up front to pay for advertisements.

Mailing Lists

Direct mail has grown in popularity in the computer age because it relies to a great extent on selecting profitable mailing lists. The computer is used primarily to perform "merge, purge, dupe-drops." For the people for whom direct mail talk is not a first language, this means to merge several lists of names together, purge double addresses (such as husband and wife), and discard duplicate addresses. For example, if a direct mail entrepreneur rents the names of American Express cardholders who live in the 75002 Zip Code and merges it with a list of Houston-area households that have recently purchased products from The Horchow Collection catalog at prices of $250 or more, there is likely to be a duplication of names. The computer can clear the list quickly. Good mailing lists include names of people who have made a significant mail order purchase within 90 days. These lists may rent for 5 cents per name, or $50 per 1000 names. To test a list, one would want to rent at least 5,000 names.

There are many list brokers and list managers, principally in the New York metropolitan area. A list manager tries to rent out the mailing lists of its clients many times every year. Many magazine publishers rent their lists frequently throughout the year and thus generate "gross equals net" dollars. That is, they generate very profitable cash from a secondary asset.

Mailing lists have become so profitable and valuable that when one acquires a company that has many subscribers, the price of the company is frequently expressed as a multiple of the number of names on the mailing list. Cable television companies, for example, trade at prices in the upper range of $1,000 to $1,500 per subscriber. Newspaper companies trade at $100 to $200 per subscriber. Prices vary with the popularity of the media. Magazines, particularly those in service sectors, were popular in the late 1980s—Time, Inc. sold *Discover* magazine in May 1987 for $26 million; *Discover* had been a big money loser for Time, yet it sold to another publisher for more than $250 per subscriber.

The point for the direct mail entrepreneur is that he or she can develop a second source of revenues once a sufficiently large customer base is developed, by renting his or her mailing list to others. A base of 2,500 names, particularly if they are high-ticket purchasers, is an appropriate size to begin with.

The "Hands of" Example

I have been tantalized by a direct mail idea that I will pass along to you as an example of the opportunities in this area. I call it the "Hands of..." opportunity, and it has two variations. The first variation is to provide a direct mail marketing service for the artists, craftsmen, sculptors, weavers, potters, and woodworkers in your community. You solve a problem for them: locating customers for their craft products. You also solve a problem for their customers: creating a directory for their craft products in your community. The more well-known your community is for its artists, the higher will be the price of the products in your mailing piece.

The arrangement that you make with the providers of the products is that you will provide a direct mail customer-finding service for them for 30 to 40 percent of the retail selling price of any and all products sold through your mailing piece for one year, automatically renewable by mutual agreement for another two to three years. You must control the orders so that the customer does not go around you, but you do not want to invest in inventory. As the orders are generated, you send an order form to the artist, who delivers the product to you, and you ship it to the customer.

A variation is to offer the same service to the merchants in your community who sell unique products, art, crafts, or indigenous products that cannot be purchased anywhere except in your community. This direct mail opportunity would solve problems for merchants in a community that has fallen on hard economic times, such as Midland, Texas, or Oklahoma City. The mailing piece can include local products, recipe books, foods, crafts, and so forth. You might even write a short story about the region and its history to romanticize the products and provide background.

You can probably launch this business without giving up your present employment. Let's examine the costs and time considerations. Initially you thumb through the Yellow Pages to obtain the names and addresses of merchants and craftspeople who sell or make unique products. This might require an evening or two. Next you spend three or four weekends calling on the merchants and craftspeople to elicit their interest in becoming a supplier to you. Thus far you have spent 30 to 50 hours and obtained, for free, the right to become an agent to market a potpourri of unique products. It will take some communications leverage on your part, because what you are doing is borrowing someone's proprietary product and trying to make money with it. But the merchants and craftspeople would not be able to mount a direct mail campaign in their spare time. They usually do not have this kind of spare time, and a mailing piece listing a variety of products and craftspeople would be more attractive to the reader.

Bearing in mind the need to shift expenses to suppliers, you then ask the merchants and craftspeople to provide camera-ready copy, with a photograph of their product or products, and size, color, and weight information, as well as prices. It has been demonstrated by the success of L.L. Bean and Horchow that one of the perceived values of shopping by mail is that the customer can obtain exact information on the weight, size, and color choices of the products. Store clerks frequently cannot answer questions put to them about the product. In the comfort of the home or office, a direct mail customer can visualize the product and its location, determine if it fits, and select the best color. With a telephone or an envelope and a stamp, the product can be ordered conveniently with a check or credit card.

You collect the camera-ready art work and take it to a printer for layout and production. Some direct mail entrepreneurs have been successful at convincing their printers to wait for payment until orders are generated. (The founders of *Psychology Today* convinced their printer to wait to be paid on their first issue—it can be done.)

You then contact a broad sampling of list managers and list brokers to discuss with them the lists they represent that might work best for your Hands of... mailing piece. Normally you would rent these different lists, each of 5,000 names of people who habitually order through the mail, people who travel to your community, and people who subscribe to *Sunset* or *Southern Living* or a similar magazine in your region that describes crafts to its readers. The objective is to mail your minicatalog to these 15,000 names to see which lists from which regions generate the most orders.

This test will cost $750 for the mailing lists, $1,500 for third-class mail, and a negotiated amount for printing. When the orders are received you can then test your ability to handle and process them, obtain the product from the vendor, and then ship to the customer. You can test whether your entrepreneurial idea is a good one by telephoning a handful of customers to see what they like about the minicatalog, which products most appeal to them and why, and what they would like to see more of, less of, or not see again. It would be up to you to review the results of your test mailing to see in which direction you should point. Like Marines landing on the beach, deal-makers fire in all directions and then move in the direction of the things that fall. Finally, the tests provide you with useful information for modifying the minicatalog and ensuring that the vendors have products available and that shipping and handling systems are in place to handle 1,000 orders in 60 days.

You then rent 100,000 names and incur an aggregate expense of $20,000 to kick off your new venture. If the test mailing generated 100 orders at $200 per order, and if you received 30 percent of the cash, then you have $6,000 of the $20,000 in hand. The balance of the $20,000 can be raised by renting the list and mailing out the minicatalogs serially, perhaps at the rate of 10,000 per month.

If your response rate is 2 percent and if the average order size is $200, then 10,000 pieces mailed will generate $40,000 in orders—of which you will receive $12,000, given our assumptions. Your costs per 10,000-name mailing would be $2,000, plus certain labor costs for stuffing and mailing. So over a six-month period you mail out 100,000 pieces and, at a 2 percent response rate, generate $400,000 in sales, of which you receive $120,000 and your merchants and craftspeople receive $280,000. If there are 50 vendors in your Hands of... catalog, the average sale per vendor in the first mailing is $5,600—a sale the vendor would not have had without your entrepreneurial vision.

You have done much more, however. You have launched a new company with $120,000 of customers' money. That is attractive deal-making.

Using Customers' Money for Newsletters

There is no simpler business to launch on customers' advance payments than a newsletter business. The first deal-maker to make money in a new industry is the newsletter publisher. The service he or she provides is to identify the problem that the new entrepreneurs of the industry are intent on solving. Frequently, the newsletters grow into magazines or branch into seminars, cassettes from seminars, or conventions.

Many new markets are in need of careful and frequent identification of their problems. When the women's liberation market was relatively new, the problems created by male chauvinism were identified by *Ms.* magazine. *Ms.* is a fine, upbeat publication that indexes problems and problem-solving solutions each month in the complex area of the changing role of women. *Ms.* created this market, built up a demand curve for liberating products, and has sold books, tapes, and services into it. *Ms.* grew quickly to over 100,000 subscribers and with its strong cash flow entered the facilities management business. A large truck manufacturer paid *Ms.* over six figures to provide it with advice in the redesign of its cab to sell more women and team drivers. The fee must have been very profitable, perhaps equal to several months' profits at the magazine.

Other markets come to mind as likely candidates for newsletters as a base for launching new products or services, such as the nutrition market, with follow-on nutrition products; alternative energy markets; the genetic engineering market; the home computer market; the home video market; and others. The definition of a new market that will be of interest to entrepreneurs and venture capitalists is one with at least three newsletters.

Aside from the newsletters' ability to generate cash up front on a subscription basis or monthly on a newsstand basis, a newsletter itself is very inexpensive to initiate. You need a mailing list and a printer willing to prepare many postcards. An optimistic publisher is able to convince the owner of the mailing list and the mail order printer to be paid out of initial subscriptions.

Financing a New Company
Through Direct Response

Direct response has become an increasingly popular method of financing a new company, given the proliferation of credit cards and the growing reluctance of shoppers to drive to a mall to make purchases. The necessary ingredients for the launch are consumer product, a high gross profit margin, and a retail price of less than $50. The direct response method involves advertising the product heavily and soliciting orders by way of mail order (advertisements in newspapers or magazines), direct mail (mailings to rented lists of names), or other media, and then applying the net receipts to produce and deliver the products that are ordered. A primary example of the direct response method of financing a new company is the "Oldies-but-Goodies" type of record publishing. In most instances the albums advertised on television have not been produced at the time of the advertisement, but will be upon receipt of the thousands of small checks that will pour in following the advertisement.

You have probably read the direct response advertisements of Joe Sugarman, the Northbrook, Illinois, entrepreneur who founded JS&A. JS&A advertisements in airline magazines and financial journals for small electronic gadgets are, in a word, masterful. More important, they work. For entrepreneurs who have developed high-profit consumer electronic products that can be produced to sell for around $50 or less, JS&A and comparable mail-order companies such as The Sharper Image will market the product. Their share of the pie will vary from 35 percent to 50 percent of selling price.

Deal Money from Stuffers

Credit card companies, oil companies, and department stores that offer credit cards to their customers often send product offers (called "stuffers") to their customer lists in their monthly billing envelopes. This is a widely used means for selling small appliances, giftware, housewares, decorative accessories, and art prints. One of the typical pricing methods is for the credit card issuer to incur all the marketing costs in exchange for 50 percent of the retail selling price. For art prints that are marked up about 800 percent, the value of a Sears mailing to 20 million Sears credit card customers is extraordinary. Assume that an artist charged you $10,000 for a drawing and that you could reproduce it for $5 apiece and sell the prints for $40. Assume further that a department store stuffed your offer into 2 million envelopes and that 1 percent of the recipients (20,000) ordered the print. Your revenues would be $800,000, of which the department store would keep $400,000. Your costs would be $100,000 for a net profit before taxes of $290,000. Even with a one half of 1 percent response, you would profit handsomely.

Whether you act as a direct mail intermediary for other people's products or develop a product line yourself and sell it by direct mail, your initial investment requirements of time and money are minimal. You use customers' money to launch your company.

ASSEMBLING YOUR NETWORK OF HELPERS

To close deals you need to involve many helpers—a network of allies, as it were. Such networking, however, goes beyond advice and contacts into the concept of deal money. Deal money means making a handful of people responsible for portions of your deal, whereby the cooperation of each person involved in the deal is essential to the company's debt. The larger and more ambitious the undertaking, the larger the network of people that you must pull together to help you. There is no deal too small, however, to obviate your need for deal money. Even the Hands of... launch requires deal money. The printer is a player, as are the list brokers and the attorney who incorporates your company. Even the economic development director in your community who leads you to vendors and finds some local grant money is a player. Your banker is a player, and he or she should be informed of the kind of cash flow that your company anticipates. The banker may be willing to provide a loan secured by your mailing list when you begin to expand the catalog in the second or third year.

There are certain people you should contact to join the deal who will "loan" you a resource today in consideration for a future return. Let's assume your new company will benefit your community in some way—through jobs, generating income (which means income taxes), recruiting people into the community, new construction, and ancillary employment. A study made by United States Congressman Ed Zchau, Republican–California, several years ago showed that every new job created by an entrepreneur leads to one new service job in the community—teacher, beautician, auto repairman, and so on. This fact, misunderstood by most economists who believe mistakenly that only big companies create jobs, will bring you more success in borrowing resources from members of your deal circle than any other single statement you can make. Your new company and its derived economic benefits are reciprocal gifts that you give to your community. The community's gift to you is the resource base from which you select members and components of a deal circle that can help your launch. Some communities are richer in resources than are others, and you may wish to relocate to one of the communities more responsive to entrepreneurs. But in many instances moving is not necessary.

Economic Development Director

You may want to begin with the local (or regional, or state) economic development director, whose job it is to know how to pull people together to get new companies launched and new jobs created. Economic development directors feel responsible to help all entrepreneurs equitably. However, they may have a particular park that they wish to put tenants into or abandoned plants that they want to fill with equipment and workers, and you should recognize that this is their goal, their means of gaining recognition and promotion. But the economic development directors also know where the money is in the state or in the financial institutions and pension funds and insurance companies within the state.

Local Insurance Agent

Insurance companies buy risks and invest or loan money to entrepreneurs either directly or through venture capital funds that they invest in. As the "kingpin," you should certainly purchase some insurance on your life, splitting the benefits between your spouse and the stockholders of your company. It is important to purchase business insurance so that if anyone is damaged due to negligence by one of your employees or is injured by tripping on your rug, you do not sustain a loss. Directors' and officers' liability insurance may not be available to a start-up, or may be too expensive, but you should ask about it. Explain to the insurance agent that you will purchase the relevant policies as soon as you raise some up-front cash. The insurance agent knows many wealthy people, and he or she may open the door for you because doing so may make you a customer of means yourself.

Stockbrokers

Including the local stockbroker is another way to gain access to deal money. Stockbrokers deal in risk as well, and may lead you to some seed capital investors. When I was launching Mesa Diagnostics in Los Alamos, New Mexico, a technology transfer from Los Alamos National Laboratory, I visited with a stockbroker from the local Prudential-Bache office. He told me about Pru-Tech, the R&D limited partnership fund that Prudential-Bache had formed with $100 million of customers' capital. Several months later, Mesa Diagnostics received a $7.5 million funding from Pru-Tech. The stockbroker can introduce you to sources of deal money in consideration for opening a money market account for your new company in the future to manage the company's idle cash.

Bankers

Another logical start-up ally might seem to be your local banker. But commercial bankers are risk averse, and it is unlikely that they will provide loans to you to start your new company unless there is hard collateral and an obvious source of repayment. Nonetheless, your new company will need a bank account, and it will be worth your while to take your banker to lunch to fill him or her in on your plans. You will need references and sponsorship, and a banking reference is among the best.

An "incubator" is a physical facility that houses prestart-up companies and provides them with assistance in formulating their business plan. In some communities an incubator is developed by a local university, laboratory, or other institution. Dr. Fran Jabara of Wichita, Kansas, has for 38 years been a quiet, yet enormously effective deal-maker in that haven of entrepreneurship. Wichita has spawned Pizza Hut, Inc.; Rent-A-Center, Inc.; AFG Industries, Inc.; Schepler's, Inc.; Lear Jet Corporation; and the Young Entrepreneurs' Organization. Thanks to Dr. Jabara's groundwork, launching a new company is relatively easy in Wichita.

THE PYRAMID METHOD OF TACKLING
A NEW MARKET

Assume we have an entrepreneur who has ideas for solving the problem of corporate drug and chemical dependency. Assume also that the entrepreneur was until recently a human resources officer of a large corporation and that she became aware of dependencies among male middle managers placed under a great deal of pressure. Some wives and children complained that they could not sustain meaningful relationships. Some children's schoolwork slipped badly. The middle manager and his wife found solace in drink or drugs. Wrenched by the notion of Corporate America being torn apart emotionally by drug and chemical dependency, the human resources officer suggested to her employer that the families receive counseling.

The corporation permitted her to do family counseling with employees to learn some antidotes for the problem. She became experienced in the field and began to make progress within her corporation, making senior management more sensitive to this issue. The human resources officer was making progress until the day her boss left the corporation and her activity was expunged by the new boss. The new boss's attitude was simply that if an employee was abusing drink or drugs, he wasn't a team player and should be canned.

The human resources officer resigned in order to start a corporate chemical dependency counseling business.

Building the Marketing Pyramid

The entrepreneur began her new endeavor by sketching a pyramid of the market, which appears in Exhibit 4.2 and is based on the pyramid method of problem formulating. Her object is to convert as many of the 2,000 human resources officers as possible into clients. The goal is to widen the pyramid at the top. This is done by making the market aware of the problem.

Newsletter Start-Up

Many entrepreneurs begin business with a newsletter. It is a unique device to heighten awareness. The corporate chemical dependency

Exhibit 4.2
MARKET PYRAMID FOR CORPORATE CONSULTING BUSINESS

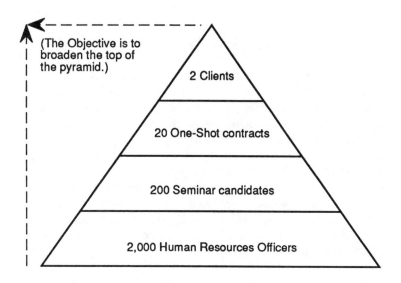

(The Objective is to broaden the top of the pyramid.)

2 Clients

20 One-Shot contracts

200 Seminar candidates

2,000 Human Resources Officers

newsletter is offered to 2,000 human resources officers on a subscription basis, 10 issues for $120. If 400 subscribe, the entrepreneur has $48,000 in launch capital. It is possible to attract advertisers for a newsletter, but this particular newsletter does not immediately suggest any good ideas for ads.

Seminar Marketing

Two or three months of publishing go by. The entrepreneur reports on the subject from every vantage point imaginable: the human angle, the legal angle, the moral angle, and so forth. In the fourth month, believing that some of her subscribers are ready to meet to discuss the issue, she announces a seminar. For $500 the human resources officers can meet in Chicago for two days of panel discussion and lectures by psychologists and psychiatrists. Checks are received from 75 human resources officers, or $37,500 in revenues. The entrepreneur spends $10,000 on a first-class seminar—good lunches, good speakers, and a comfortable hotel (the guests pay for lodging). She makes this back by selling tapes of the seminar to nonattendees for $75 each.

Growth of Dependency Counseling Business

From the seminar the entrepreneur gets 75 leads from corporations who are beginning to understand the extent of their problem. She offers each of them a small consulting assignment: one day's analysis for $1,000. Twenty corporations sign up over the next three months, for further revenues of $20,000.

From these 20 consulting assignments the entrepreneur is awarded two performance contracts. She will counsel with all families that are suffering from the chemical dependency problem and recommend to the corporation whether or not they can be salvaged with treatment. The contracts are worth $25,000 each, plus expenses for one year. Thus, after the first 12 months of operation, the entrepreneur has generated the following revenues:

Performance Contracts	$ 50,000
Consulting Assignments	20,000
Seminars, Tapes	47,500
Newsletter	48,000
Total Revenues	$ 165,000

In the second year, the newsletter could double its revenues. There can be 2 seminars, one on each coast, another 20 consulting assignments, and 4 new performance contracts. As revenues approach $300,000, the entrepreneur hires someone to publish the newsletter, assist with the seminars, and keep the books.

Entering the third year, the entrepreneur hires one of the human resource officers she has befriended and brings him into the company as a coworker. Growth continues, and the entrepreneur begins to find other ways to permit growth of revenues without sacrificing quality.

The pyramid method for tackling a new market that needs to be more problem-aware is an entrepreneurial creation. For entrepreneurs in search of new markets to attack, the *Newsletter of Newsletters*, available in most large city libraries, suggests pyramids in search of entrepreneurs.

MAKING THE MOST OF OPPORTUNITIES

If you ever thought about becoming a deal person, pick your audience and pick your problem, because the opportunities will never be greater. Wherever there is a big business or government bureaucracy attempting to provide a solution, dozens of entrepreneurial solutions exist. Wherever there are hundreds of mom-and-pop operations doing their thing inefficiently, entrepreneurial managers are needed to bring them together to concentrate their energy and talent. Now, if we could fit entrepreneurs into the right problems, capital and time could be conserved.

Each of us can make money when we rely on our skills, but when we are lured away from employing our skills to their maximum by curiosity or vanity, this usually requires us to raise outside capital in amounts far greater than we ever imagined needing. On the other hand, duplicating or replicating our skills rather than our egos usually requires raising smaller amounts of outside money.

Deal-making is doing *some one thing* extremely well. Not two things. Thus, each potential deal-maker must find that one thing that he or she can do very well and do it. If the wrong problem is picked, the result will be failure. Finding the right problem means finding the right audience as well. Just who is your audience?

In this age of transactions, the simple seems to offer more solutions than the complex.

CHAPTER **5**

JUST ASK: HOW THE RIGHT QUESTIONS CAN PUT YOU IN CONTROL OF THE DEAL

CONTROL THE DEAL MEETING WITH QUESTIONS

We move now from strategy to tactics; from preparing the meal to setting the table. Let's assume everything you have learned to this point has enabled you to craft a doable deal. That is, your deal solves a need; a network of key people, each of whom has something to gain and something to lose, been identified and contacted; the obstacles or tollgates have been circumnavigated; and upfront money has been raised by leveraging assets or cash flow channels. Now it is time to get to the meeting and ask for the commitment.

VIEW YOUR DEAL FROM THE OUTSIDE IN

Many people with deals in their attaché cases and a speech in their hearts charge into a meeting with an immense amount of *chutzpah*, buckets of insouciance, and an aplomb that seems to the buyer significantly greater in magnitude than the deal itself. The deal is what is important, not the seller of the deal. Too much cocksuredness can kill an otherwise good deal.

To be sure, you want to appear confident to the buyer, but it is the buyer's ego identity that you want to somehow lift hydraulically in the deal meeting, not your own. You want the buyer to feel extraordinarily proud that he has selected your deal to invest in or buy, not yourself. To do this, you must view the deal from the outside in. This means trying to put yourself in the buyer's shoes.

But you do not know what shoes your buyer is wearing unless you ask questions. In the direct mail or database marketing businesses, data on customers is collected via bounceback and warranty cards. Enter a consumer product manufacturer's contest in which your name, address, telephone number, age (or birthday) and gender are requested, and the manufacturer has a lot of information about you and tens of thousands like you to improve its target market. Buy a house or a car, and a lot of financial information is in a public hall of records for dozens of companies to access, merge with census tracts, and collect an unusually large amount of information about you. Database marketers obtain this information by asking questions. After they ask their questions, they prepare the pitch.

This should apply to a one-on-one deal meeting as well. Begin the conversation and control the flow of dialogue with questions. "Have you invested in deals that address this particular market?" is a logical question. The purpose of it is to determine your ground; you do not want to present a deal to a buyer who may have already bought a similar competitive deal. But the question reaches for a much broader answer. You can learn from the answer if the buyer has a generic interest in your deal or a prejudice against it. You can follow a path from the buyer's answer into the dollar amount of investments of this type that the buyer has made in the last year, his or her degree of literacy about the area that you are addressing, and the buyers' need to be educated about your particular opportunity.

"What is your typical investment size?" is another fair question to ask early on in the presentation. You want to know—indeed you are *entitled* to know—the house rules. This means the average size of investment, the number of deals done per year, whether or not the investor invests with others, and the typical length of the investor's due diligence process are all realistic bytes of data that you need to qualify the investor or customer.

Interspersed throughout, of course, is your presentation. You provide the headline, the problem or need that you are addressing—the sub-headline, a succinct description of your solution—and a summary of the strategy for conveying the solution to the problem. You summarize the track records of your team and key players, and then ask another question: "Which of these points would you like me to amplify?" This is a fair and important question because the buyer may not have heard clearly everything you've said; or the buyer may be interested in the mechanics of the solution rather than the broad brush painting of the opportunity. His or her answer will permit you to respond with a little more depth, but quickly return to your questions.

"What was your all-time greatest investment—the one you would like to do again?" This is an off-putting question, but most buyers will answer it because it compliments their acumen and buying judgment. And it is an important question to have the answer to because you sincerely want to know the things that make your buyer feel good.

There are many questions such as these that you should use in the deal meeting to open up the buyer. Listen to a good gospel preacher before you go into the meeting. Many of them have an uncanny ability to bring their audiences out of their shells and into the gospel message by making every second or every third statement a question. Gospel preachers have more competition for their message than you or I do. Their message is not unique. But their presentations are among the best you will ever see performed.

THE TACTICS OF CLOSING: AN OVERVIEW

There is a point in the movement of a deal from conception to closing at which a deal meeting occurs. At this meeting, the buyer is most likely prepared to commit. If he or she is not interested, a turndown would have occurred earlier. However, if the buyer lacks the authority to commit, then what you perceived to be a deal meeting will in reality be a *messenger meeting*; that is, a meeting at which you communicate your most cogent and winning points to someone who will subsequently carry them to a committee for final approval. The messenger meeting is as important as the deal meeting if you won't be permitted to meet the full committee. Thus, the messenger meeting should be accorded all the importance of the deal meeting.

Ask the messenger if his recommendations are generally accepted by the committee; if the committee goes into detail with each deal submitted to it or merely "rubber stamps" the messenger's recommendations; whether or not the messenger is a major producer of deals for the buyer; if the messenger is allowed to have a voice at the committee meetings to explain or persuade in order to get his deals closed. With the answers to this information you will know for whom you are preparing your *deal sheet*. If it is for the full committee to read and consider, then it will have to be longer and more detailed to serve as a stand-in for you at the committee meeting.

Prepare the deal sheet in order to make all the points that you want the committee to know about. If the deal sheet is left to the messenger to prepare, something may be left out or the major points may not be amplified. You must control the deal very carefully at this point, and that means asking a lot of questions to learn as much about the buyer as possible.

This is an overview of the tactics of closing. Let's now go through the process of closing from finding the buyers, to eliciting their interest, to getting the meeting, to closing the deal at the meeting.

SELLING YOURSELF AS A "DOER"

Selling the deal begins the moment you enter the prospect's room. Enter quickly and confidently with a glowing smile, an extended hand, and an unexpected remark such as "Thank you for seeing me. Sorry to be late—we've just completed our biggest month in history..." or "a major order from General Energy Corporation,"... or "a session with our patent counsel...." Thus, the first impression is that you are a "doer."

One entrepreneur I know always says, "It's done" as he enters the lender's or investor's office for the first time. "It's done" is a surprising remark. My entrepreneur friend claims that it is the single best opener because it is completely unexpected, and it makes you look like a doer, an accomplisher—and it subjectively encourages the lender to do something with you also. If you are part of an entrepreneurial team, the two of you could enter the room, one saying to the other, "It's done!" and then introducing yourselves gleefully to the lender. Chances are the lender will ask "What's done?" Your verbal presentation then begins on a positive note of accomplishment. Your response to the "What's Done?" question could inspire the lender to write something in the margin of a page of your plan. (More on writing during the meeting and its significance further on.)

DRESS AND BODY LANGUAGE

Dress is important in selling a credit. When a lender considers whether or not to grant a loan, in the back of his or her mind is a nagging concern that the entrepreneur may lack the judgment to spend the money wisely. This concern is definitely not major once a positive decision has been reached, but the entrepreneur's appearance could affect a decision just enough to skew it from slightly bullish to slightly bearish. Hence, the entrepreneur's clothing should suggest conservatism more than liberalism, risk aversion more than risk taking, caution rather than devil-may-care optimism. The lender unconsciously looks for some outward and visible sign that the entrepreneur will be a wise steward of the institution's money.

Speak Yiddish and Dress British

E. Roe Stamps, a partner in the venture capital firm of Summit Ventures, says that successful entrepreneurs usually "speak Yiddish and dress British." That is, they incorporate colorful Yiddish terms of commerce, of which there are many, while dressing like Saville Row bankers.

In negotiating the technology transfer of a flow cytometry product in 1983 from Los Alamos National Laboratory, I resorted to Yiddish phrases in order to relax the head of the Department of Life Sciences, whom I had to convince in order to obtain the rights to the product. Neither he nor I had ever done a technology transfer, nor was there precedent for us to follow. To show that I was sincere and aboveboard and that I could raise the money to pay the lab, I needed to relax him to gain his cooperation.

Sensing that he might know Yiddish, I said, "Let's put *touchas offen tish*." He broke out in gales of laughter and began to cooperate. The transfer resulted in one of the more innovative medical diagnostic products of recent years, developed by Mesa Diagnostics, Inc.

What I said to him was: "Let's put our rear ends on the table," or (figuratively), "Let's open up with one another."

As for "dressing British," that is relative. A Saville Row suit would not go over in Texas or Los Angeles, though it might in Boston or San Francisco. Here are some dress tips for the entrepreneur.

1. *New England:* Dark blue suit, blue shirt, fairly small print paisley tie, lace-up shoes.

2. *New York:* Gray pinstripe suit, blue shirt, red and blue striped tie, lace-up shoes or conservative loafers.

3. *Chicago and Industrial Midwest:* Gray or dark brown suit, dark tie, lace-up shoes. Give appearance of being ready to slap a hard hat on your head and tramp through a foundry right after the meeting.

4. *South and Southwest:* Light gray or brown suit, any color shirt except white, bright tie, lace-up shoes or conservative loafers.

5. *Los Angeles:* Similar to the South and Southwest, except colors should be coordinated, and loafers may be tasseled.

6. *San Francisco:* Dark blue suit, white shirt, bright tie, lace-up shoes or conservative loafers.

Like her male counterpart, the female deal-maker will want to look confident but not intimidating. There are enough unconsciously held barriers to women in business without adding the distraction of inappropriate dress. Women should follow the regional guidelines above, translating suits and ties to simply tailored suits and scarves worn with conservative shoes. Jewelry should be plain and understated. Since there are relatively few women involved in finance and entrepreneurial ventures at the time of this writing, it is hard to make generalizations about women's dress and, in turn, there are no set formulas expected by lenders.

What you wear can establish a subliminal link with the investor. Lenders vicariously adopt some of the plans, dreams, and aspirations of the entrepreneurs to whom they lend money. It is inevitable that the lender will reflect, "Do I see a part of myself in that entrepreneur? Do we share common goals? Are we at all alike?" It is in this area that dress plays a role—albeit secondary to the substance of the conversation, but important in that the entrepreneur should present an appearance more suggestive to handling money wisely than of going to a ball game.

WORDS AND BODY LANGUAGE

Good use of body language and word choice are important when selling your proposal. Select the most comfortable seat near the lender, and at all times sit straight and slightly forward. Never lean back or become relaxed. If the lender sits behind a desk, you should sit in front of the desk and place your material on the desk in front of you. The entrepreneur should never appear at ease. The subject is money, and that is not a casual topic. One entrepreneur with whom I have worked believes that the entrepreneur should appear very ill at ease and uncomfortable.

One of the best credit-selling meetings I attended involved a commercial bank officer and an entrepreneur whose company, in bankruptcy proceedings at the time, had just completed its second year of operations with revenues of $75,000. The entrepreneur was a skilled salesperson, and he pulled out all the stops in the empathy game. He pretended he was too hot and asked if he might remove his jacket. It was the South, so jacket removal was acceptable. He put the jacket over the arm of his chair and then tugged at his collar, still looking like a fully dressed man in a steam room. All the while he was describing his business and its prospects once it obtained financing. In the meantime, he coordinated collar tugs with knocking his jacket to the floor, picking it up, pushing it down, picking it up, shifting around, folding and unfolding the jacket, and finally letting it fall and stepping on it. At that point the bemused lender left his seat and came over to the agitated entrepreneur, ostensibly to see his material more closely, but in fact, to put the entrepreneur at ease. Once that was accomplished, a bridge financing was put together.

Another style is that of the deal-maker who becomes so excited about the prospects for her company that she has to stand up and walk around. The excitement, if you will, causes her to leave her seat. While standing she has two basic moves to employ: "the grip" and "the stroll." The grip involves holding tightly to the back of a chair for support and reassurance, and the stroll is simply an animated walk around the lender's office, one hand in a jacket pocket, the other moving furiously to stress various points. An apology then follows, on the order of, "I'm sorry, but I get so excited sometimes I can't keep my seat." Sounds corny? It would be if everyone did it. But many entrepreneurs are frightened in meetings with lenders and sit in a near-fetal position as far from the lender's desk as possible, hoping desperately for success but unable to put their bodies into the effort.

The best deal-makers use their hands in syncopation with their voice. Billy Graham slices the air up and down and side to side. Oral Roberts, while saying, "Let me help you—let me give to you," rolls his hands outward to his audience. Reverend Ike shoots his bejeweled hands skyward. Johnny Carson, who sells shyness, leaves his hands in his pockets and brings them out Jack Benny-style to underscore surprise. The list of "handtalkers" is endless, and much can be learned from watching them. For entrepreneurs who are poor speakers, I recommend hiring a speech tutor or coach.

There are dozens of body language signs to watch for in a meeting with a lender. If a lender's arms and legs are folded or crossed your message is not being received; your listener's mind is closed to your proposal. If the arms and legs unfold, it shows a quickening of interest. A listener who leans back with hands behind the head and legs apart is saying, "Sell me, I'm yours."

It is possible to effect a positive change in the listener's body language by a number of actions on your part. For example, you can push toward his or her hands things that have to be reached for in order to receive and examine. If the product you manufacture is small enough to bring with you, you can place that in easy reach of the lender. You can even push the product off the desk to untangle your audience's feet; he or she will have to get up in order to retrieve it.

If you are a deal-making team, one of you should take out a pencil and write during the meeting. This encourages the listener to also take note by opening up the hands and arms. Excessive body movement on your part will tend to open up the lender; it is instinctive to want to get in motion with someone in motion.

Never use the word "problem" in a meeting with a lender. Avoid sentences like, "Here's our problem." "Our problem is this," or "We have a cash flow problem." Lenders already have problems in their portfolios, and they don't want more of them. If they think you will become a problem, they will turn you down. Always bring lenders solutions, not problems.

Avoid street language, such as "con," as in "We were conned by a supplier." Avoid inferences to crime, fraud, felony, dishonesty, and, if possible, avoid discussing litigation or government action regarding your business. Such references raise the specter of uncertainty and business interruption, or the possible embarrassing—and painful—loss of the lender's money.

I have vivid memories of a lender's face turning from smiles to frowns when an entrepreneur, who was just about to get financed, launched into a crime story replete with an impersonation of a thug. The story was about a meeting the entrepreneur accidentally had with a "street lender," and although it was humorous, it placed the lender in the same category by association and also indicated that the entrepreneur was stupid enough or hard-pressed enough to have had this kind of meeting. The lender dreams of dealing with Rockefellers, Watsons, and Perots, but since they do not need money, the lender wants at least to deal with people who act like them—proud, self-reliant, honest, competent, and absolutely right.

WHEN THE BUYER SELLS:
KEY WORDS TO LISTEN FOR

If you listen carefully, you can hear a deal closing by the words and phrases the buyer uses and the ones he or she leaves out. Let's examine some of the key buyer words and phrases that indicate he or she likes the deal.

You have struck a lode of interest in your deal when the buyer says, "What would you like to know about us?"

She has warmed to the idea that she may be doing business with you, and it is time for you to know the buyer and her people, policies, and portfolio.

You respond, of course, with something that will move the conversation further along in this direction so that you can eventually ask the buyer for a check or commitment. An appropriate response would be, "I would like to get to know your firm better as we progress, so let's begin at the beginning."

The "as we progress" is the critical part of your response because the process of closing is like a musical score; it has a form and a rhythm and moves along at an observable cadence.

"I would like to learn as much as I can about your firm, and I'm sure I will have the occasion to do that at future meetings," is much too pushy and disrupts the cadence. After all, the buyer just moments ago put on his or her seller's hat, and you can't very well assume that he or she has checkbook in hand.

"I would like to learn more about your firm," is too brief an answer. It shows a very tepid interest on your part, and what's worse, you miss the opening to financing in a comment about turning today's meeting into an affair.

Encouraging the Buyer to Sell

To see where you stand with a prospective buyer, assuming he has not uttered the magical words of the previous section, you can ask if he or she would not mind telling you something about his or her firm. If the buyer responds by handing you a brochure about the firm without embroidering it, you may have been given a polite turndown.

As you accept the brochure from the buyer, respond politely and turn to a section of the brochure that is substantive, rather than a puff piece. For instance, if you are handed the buyer's annual report or financial statements, turn to the *Notes to the Financial Statements.* There is usually more substantial information in the Notes than in the numbers, and if something catches your eye that is similar to your company's condition, you should mention it. This might be the buyer's accounting firm—"We are thinking of using Coopers & Lybrand as our auditor. Is it possible to ask you for an introduction to the firm?"—or the buyer's investment in software that it is amortizing over five years—"We plan to expense our software rather than amortize it. Even though you amortize yours, isn't expensing software the preferred accounting treatment for start-ups?"—or refer to the buyer's employee profit-sharing plan—"If we are a successful investment, it appears from Note G that the employees of your firm would benefit through the profit-sharing plan." There are many hooks to grab onto if the buyer presents you with an annual report.

FIND OUT WHO MAKES THE DECISIONS

You can lead the buyer's decision-making process and the members of its decision-making committee once you are given a brochure or annual report that lists the members of management. Buyer brochures typically include group pictures of the board of directors, the executive committee, and division heads. Annual reports frequently have management names, and sometimes names and photographs.

You can raise the topic of the decision-making process in one of several ways. First, you can refer to the Chief Executive Officer by name, point to his picture or name in the brochure, and ask, "Does a project such as mine typically go to Mr. Johnson for a decision, or to the Executive Committee?"

This question should evoke an informative response, such as "No. The New Ventures Division can approve deals up to $5 million. Above that, they go to the Executive Committee."

Assuming your deal is $5 million or less, you should then ask the buyer: "Who are the members of the New Ventures Division who will vote on my deal, and will I get an opportunity to meet with them and present my story?"

This question should also prompt an informative answer, if asked tactfully. Some buyers prefer to perform due diligence on a deal by themselves and then take on the responsibility for selling it to the decision-making committee. Others prefer to prepare the seller for his presentation to the committee by suggesting an outline and deal sheet to be prepared in advance, and allowing time for a one-hour presentation several weeks into the future after the buyer is finished analyzing the deal and is comfortable with it.

FIVE KEY QUESTIONS TO ASK AT THE DEAL MEETING

The key to moving your deal along from the buyer through the decision-making process, to the deal meeting at the decision-making committee, is *to control the conversation with questions.*

Question everything. Don't presume anything. Ask the buyer as many questions as you can think of that are reasonable and material, or that lead to a material point. The ones you must know the answers to at the first meeting are:

1. Does this deal fit into your criteria?
2. Have you done a deal such as this?
3. What is the decision-making process?
4. Do I present the deal to the committee or do you carry the ball?
5. When does the decision-making committee meet next, and can my deal be put on the agenda?

These are gut questions. Successful deal-makers ask them and keep asking them because to do so allows one to gain and maintain control of the decision-making process.

Listening for Keys

In order to make certain that you hear everything that is said at a deal meeting, it is best to take a teammate with you who props a legal pad on his or her lap and writes down everything that the buyer says. The notes can be reviewed later to look for key words, phrases, and a "to do" list if the buyer gives you one.

Buyers frequently do not use direct turndown language. Rather, they use subtle phrases such as "We may have an issue with your pricing" or "We once lost money on a deal in your field" or "One of the committee members has had a lack of fondness for this kind of deal." Whereas you may be selling very hard and may miss these apparent badinages, they could be extremely important, and your teammate who is busy listening to the buyer should surely catch them.

Clarity Upfront

One of the mistakes that deal people sometimes make is *cognitive dissonance*, or hearing what they want to hear. This happens because of the innate optimism, and the can-do attitude of deal-makers. This failing underscores the need to have a second person at all deal meetings. It tempers the optimism of the deal-maker and introduces the concept of clarity.

All business is based on *trust*. For instance, when you write a check in payment of goods or services, you have written a promise to pay. If the merchant, on the other hand, takes your cash in consideration for the delivery of goods in a week or a month, he or she has promised to tender product for payment received. However, sometimes payment is delayed or the shipment is incorrect; the merchant demands more money; or the relationship breaks down in other ways. The cause of this breakdown, except for instances of fraud or deceit, is a lack of clarity upfront.

In the deal-making business, the need for clarity is even greater than for simple kinds of business transactions. This is because deals are complex—as my lawyer friend Herbert B. Max says about leveraged buyouts, "If they were easy, everyone would be doing them." They involve many people who come together in different phases and stages, whose roles are critical in making the entire deal happen. If you hear the buyer say something that makes you think he or she is *in* on terms you can accept, but in fact he or she isn't, then you will have spent time and money needlessly. You may even feel you have a cause for legal action; but put that aside, because the damages you think the buyer cost you in most cases will be less than your legal fees.

To avoid missteps and bad feelings, listen very carefully and ask questions about anything that is not clear to you.

A deal closer must also answer five questions perched in the cerebrum of every buyer:

1. How much can I make?
2. How much can I lose?
3. How do I get my money out?
4. Who else is in the deal?
5. Who says you are any good?

The fifth question brings us to the subject of endorsement. It is critical that a third party place its imprimatur on your deal. The third party can take many forms or shapes: a major customer, a foreign licensee who has bought rights, projections done by a Big-6 accounting firm, a board of directors made up of captains of industry, a well regarded consultant's opinion that your product will actually work, or a former senior official or well-known person who has agreed to work for your company. If you cannot achieve third-party endorsements of this quality, the next best thing is publicity.

6

THE IMPORTANCE OF ENDORSEMENTS

A third-party endorsement factor adds the myth of authority to the deal. Endorsement is one of the big five questions that a deal person must answer authoritatively. Advertising does not have the same effect as a third-party endorser because it is clearly a binary statement by the seller. To assist the decision-makers in arriving at a positive conclusion, the seller must arrange for publicity about the deal and its utility. There are several ways to accomplish this:

1. *Video News Releases:* stories planted on evening TV news shows that appear to be news stories.

2. *Articles in the Local Media:* Deal-makers should visit the local media while in town to call on the buyer and attempt to have a story appear prior to the decisive committee meetings.

3. *Cites in National Media:* Stories planted in national media are more difficult to accomplish, but the endorsement effect is greater.

4. *Positive Product Reviews in Trade Journals:* Having a positive story appear in the industry's principal trade journals provides an outstanding product endorsement.

DUNCAN HINES AND ROY H. PARK:
THE MASTER OF ENDORSEMENT

The master of the third-party endorsement is Roy H. Park, 77, owner
of Park Communications, Inc., Ithaca, New York, a media holding
company that owns and operates 70 publications, 14 radio stations,
and 7 television stations. This is Park's second entrepreneurial venture,
which he founded in 1962 with the proceeds of the sale of Hines-Park
Food, Inc., a company launched primarily by leveraging third-party
endorsement.

Roy H. Park was born on a farm in Dobson, North Carolina,
but his father could afford to send the four children to college. His
first job came in 1931, while Park was still a student at North
Carolina State University in Raleigh.

> "I saw a want ad in *The News and Observer*.... Someone was
> looking for a young man to do some writing. Those days many
> ads like that were come-ons, and I wanted to be sure this one
> was legitimate. The ad said to write Box 731, Raleigh, so I did.
> But I put the letter in a pink envelope. Then I went to the post
> office the next morning and waited till I saw someone take that
> pink envelope out of the box. Then I eased over and found out
> who was offering the job." It was the North Carolina Cotton Growers
> Association. Anticipating that he would be interviewed for the job,
> "I had bought myself a white cotton suit and showed up for the
> interview wearing it."

> The Cotton Growers Association was reluctant to hire him. So
> Park told his prospective employer, "I had my own typewriter and
> didn't need an office. If they'd just find me a table in a corner
> somewhere, I'd work three months for nothing."[*]

Park was hired and stayed with the Association for 11 years,
editing a magazine and taking care of public relations and sales
promotion.

One day out of the blue, Park received an invitation from Dr.
H. E. Babcock, head of a farmers' cooperative called GLF, now

---

[*] Guy Munger, "Farm Boy to Boss of a Communications Empire," *The (Raleigh,
N.C.) News and Observer*, July 29, 1984, p. 3D. Reprinted here with permission.

known as Agway, to come to Ithaca to discuss an opportunity. Park replied that he would move only to have his own business. "Young man," Dr. Babcock said, "you just bought it."

"What business did I buy?" Park asked.

"Your own ad agency," he replied. "If you need money, we'll lend it to you."[*] Dr. Babcock was also Chairman of the Board of Trustees at Cornell University.

Park successfully increased business steadily and wisely, sticking to advertising for farm businesses. He opened branches in five other cities and expanded to 125 employees in six years. Then, "I fell on my face."

"My mistake was getting into political advertising, where we did several campaigns for Tom Dewey, including appeals for the farm and small town vote in 1948."[**] When Truman beat Dewey, many clients identified Park's firm as a "loser" and switched to other agencies. Park had to come up with a new idea.

The farm cooperatives had shown Park the need for a consumer brand name of their own. Extensive market research indicated to Park the enormous consumer appeal of the name Duncan Hines. At that time, Hines was America's most famous restaurant reviewer, and the author of guidebooks that rated restaurants. Park felt that a line of Duncan Hines food products would be potent. There were two obstacles, however: (1) Hines had never permitted his name to be used, and (2) Park didn't know how to get to Hines. To prepare for his eventual meeting with Hines, Park read everything he could find on the man. He knew that Hines did not want to license his name for the wealth it might bring him. Park was introduced to Hines by a mutual friend, and Hines asked the young man: "So, you're going to make me a millionaire?" Park said, "No...[but] you can help upgrade American eating habits." Knowing also that Hines never endorsed anything, Park came to the meeting prepared with completely finished Duncan Hines labels, in full color, on dummy

---

[*] Roy H. Park, "Building a Business with No Outside Stockholders," a speech delivered November 2, 1976, at Cornell University Graduate School of Business and Public Administration. Reprinted here with permission.

[**]Ibid.

cans, cartons, and jars so that Hines could see what the concept looked like. They shook hands on a deal.

Park and Hines began product planning and testing immediately. All products underwent blind tests before market introduction to assure consistency from one product to the next. Rigid quality control standards were set by Hines, and he saw to it that the company's manufacturers met those standards.

In the meantime, Park's farm cooperative clients backed out of their commitment to pay some of the upfront costs for an interest in profits. Park had to raise money quickly, which he did from family and friends and by pulling cash out of his advertising agency and letting it slide away. To save production and shipping costs, Park mailed the labels to the packages rather than the other way around. Soon after its introduction, Duncan Hines cake mix captured a 48 percent market share. Pillsbury, Swansdown, Aunt Jemima, and Betty Crocker brands took the hit. As Parks says, "We could never outspend those giants—so we out-thought them."[*]

Duncan Hines was the first cake mix to be advertised on television. In the late 1940s, Mr. Hines acted in the commercials, which was also a first in consumer products advertising. Hines-Parks Foods was also the first company to use four-color ads in newspapers. Park also used outdoor ads to remind the housewife of the commercial she saw the previous evening on television. Park took Hines on the road, talking mayors and governors into declaring "Duncan Hines Days," and presenting him with keys to the city. The Duncan Hines Days generally ended with a big dinner, to which the governor, the mayor, city bigwigs, and the key chain store buyers were invited, along with their wives. The latter were presented with a corsage and an autographed *Duncan Hines Cookbook* on arrival. Park instructed his people to sell nothing at the party. "The next day was another story," says Park.

With distribution in 23 states and 120 different cake mixes, the Duncan Hines brand was second in sales among all brands by the mid-1950s.

---

[*] Ibid.

MARKETING BY THE ASSOCIATION ENDORSEMENT

Painters and sculptors are a class of deal-makers that have long used third-party endorsement as a motivator to sell their product. The endorsers appear in publications about the artists that list the names of museums that own the artists' work and names of well-known collectors that have purchased the artists' work. Getting into these collections requires outthinking other artists, but that has been going on since the Renaissance. Art in those days was purchased by patrons, such as the Medicis, to be displayed in their homes and in churches; no museums existed. Thus, the artists *created* endorsers, which they called associations, and made themselves members. Call this endorsement by exclusion.[*]

> Certainly the winning of a place in society was an overriding preoccupation with artists in the seventeenth century.... It was this motive that inspired their renewed efforts to put their professional association, the Academia di S. Lucia, on a sound footing.... Urban VIII... estabished (*sic*.) its absolute authority in the art world...by appointing the Pope's nephew, Cardinal Francesco Barberini, as its protector.... In 1633 the Academia was given the right to raise taxes on all the artists in Rome...which served [the] purpose giving new dignity to artists.

Strategic painters and sculptors have sought collectors who will donate their work to art museums, thus providing the artists with the required endorsement necessary to sell more art at higher and higher prices. Collectors are eager to donate art to museums both for tax purposes and to achieve the privileges and social acclaim that accompanies generous gifts to the community's art museum. As Will and Ariel Durant have written, giving art to museums is a means of "perfuming one's fortune."

The artists of the Renaissance are the founders of the strategy of third-party endorsement via an association. The strategy is simplicity

---

[*] Haskell, Francis, *Patrons and Painters*, Alfred A. Knopf, New York, 1963, pp. 17–18.

itself: After formulating your concept or solution, create an association in the form of a not-for-profit organization, then have the association set standards for the concept; these standards encompass your product and possibly exclude others.

For instance, if you create a new process for enabling cars to be fueled by the ethanol captured from landfills, immediately form the Association of Alternative Automobile Fuel Providers. Next step: Begin publishing its newsletter. Third step: Sponsor seminars to promote interest in alternative automobile fuels and explain the benefits of your product. Note how the endorsement factor can roll into multichannel marketing: endorsement—association—newsletters—seminars—back-table product sales.

PROMOTING THROUGH VIDEO NEWS RELEASES

A recent phenomenon, the video news release, is a 90-second clip on a television news show that appears to the viewers to be a news story, but in reality is a promotion for a product or service. The television station is sent a videotape by a video news release production firm and it is run on a slow news day or night, usually following national and local news stories, and before weather and sports. The video news release usually has a national "angle," such as employment, health care, or the environment, but then segues into the specific message that the promoter seeks to get across. Mobil Oil has used video news releases as has Gallo Wine and the author, in promoting one of his books on entrepreneurship, *Entrepreneurial Megabucks: The One Hundred Greatest Entrepreneurs of the Last Twenty-Five Years.*[*] It is one of the most effective promotional strategies ever devised by Madison Avenue's fertile minds.

Viewers of television news broadcasts are generally serious people who are watching the news in order to be informed. Viewers of advertising frequently tolerate the ads, or do something that diverts their attention, during the advertisement. The video news releases

---

[*] John Wiley & Sons, Inc., New York, 1987.

look like news, sound like news, and appear to be part of the news program, but in fact are a promotion paid for by the promoter, broadcast free of charge by the television station. Moreover, the costs of a video news release are pennies per viewer.

How much would you pay to have your company or its products favorably described for ninety seconds on the evening news shows in three hundred major markets? Put another way, what would you pay to reach approximately three million serious television viewers with your message? Would you pay $35,000? That's about one cent per viewer.

Video news releases are the creation of DWJ Associates, Inc., New York City. Michael Friedman, DWJ's cofounder, conceived the notion that local television stations were short of news stories. "So we went to advertisers and asked them to pay for DWJ to shoot a ninety-second news release about their products; we would make copies and send them to about three hundred stations to use as fillers." Every station doesn't run the video news releases each time, but many do, enough to bring DWJ clients such as Mobil Oil, The Tea Council, Dow Chemical, Merck, General Electric, and Durango Cookery. Even I have marketed books using this unique form of advertising.

At a cost of one cent per lead, if a fraction of 1 percent of the viewers order the product, you can find 20,000 new customers and make your investment back quickly.

CONTACTING LOCAL NEWSPAPERS

Outside endorsement for your deal, timed to appear while the buyer is making up his or her mind, can be achieved by visiting the business writers in the headquarter cities of the buyers. Assume for the moment that your deal involves shooting a movie that will involve several hundred extras. You have a choice of locations based on which community provides the most funding and other benefits. Newspaper articles that run in the cities that are in contention for the movie can help bid up the value of the project. After all, visions of several hundred jobs, if only for a short period of time, plus all the money spent locally by movie companies, is the kind of fodder that sells newspapers.

If your project involves bringing a manufacturing plant to a small community that will employ 20 people in its first year, increasing to 50 after three years, subject to funding, you should advertise in local newspapers in the communities that are being considered for the plant site. Politicians read newspapers, and they and their family members see people from the community in the supermarkets, drugstores, and waiting in line at the post office. Jobs win votes, and a favorable newspaper story can influence politicians to up the ante for a project.

Never give a story to a newspaper reporter over the telephone, but rather visit the reporter and discuss the project with him or her in some detail, making certain to point out that it is embryonic and requires funding to get off the ground. The press could accidentally print your story as *a fait accompli* unless you provide information to them in person, with an opportunity to review their understanding, or provide them with a printed press release. An optimistic or bullish story could boomerang on you, as it did on a friend of mine who told the press that he was moving a division to Tucson, Arizona, where he would employ eight people. The newspaper quoted him as saying 200 new jobs would be created, but that was the figure for his company's total payroll. He entered Tucson with a black eye, all because of a misinterpreted telephone interview.

KEEP THE HANDOUTS FLOWING

Keep some of your powder dry. Understate your capabilities. Following the initial telephone call to qualify the buyer and elicit his interest in reviewing your business plan, a fairly complete business plan is couriered in (I prefer that to mailing because it assures receipt of the package and it gives a sense of urgency to the deal) and that is followed up with a meeting. At this meeting (the first meeting as opposed to the deal meeting), you should bring several visual handouts that amplify on the business plan. Pictures are worth a thousand words.

However, do not distribute all your handouts at once.

To keep your deal at the top of the buyer's stack, send a continual
flow of handouts and information pieces.

Yours is not the only deal the buyer is reviewing. Indeed, as
soon as you leave the buyer's office, another seller will enter and
much of your presentation will become blurred and forgotten. Plus,
when the seller leaves the buyer's office, his or her deal will be
stacked on top of yours. Then the two or three deals that arrive the
next day will be stacked on top of these, and within five days
following your meeting, there will be 12 to 15 deals stacked up on
top of yours.

Thus, when you telephone the buyer to assess his or her reaction
to the meeting that you had a week ago, he or she will need a
crane to lift the stack of deals off yours to try to remember what
you talked about. To prevent this from happening, you want the
buyer to keep your deal at the top of the heap by reading about it
once every few days on one of your handouts.

PROMISES, PROMISES—MAKE SURE
YOU FOLLOW THROUGH

When you are at a meeting with the buyer giving your oral presentation,
create several opportunities to say that you will send something to
him or her. He or she may ask for an industry study, or about your
patent or copyright. Take this opportunity to say, "I will send that
in to you," or "I have that in my office, but I'll be glad to send
it to you." Then pause and write a note on a small pad that you
carry with you for writing down important notes. The buyer will
see that you are taking his or her needs seriously.

You may even volunteer to send additional data such as more
current financial statements or copies of contracts. Jot these notes
down as well to give them the ring of importance. Then when you
send in five or six handouts to the buyer it will not appear to be
overkill because you promised that you would do it. And it will
probably take five or six separate mailings of supplemental information

to move the deal from "possibly interesting" to "possible deal," at which time you are invited back for the *close*.

Your cover letters on subsequent mail-ins should be very brief because you are not overtly selling at this point. But these should convey the point that you are fulfilling your *promise* to get back to the buyer with the information on the Gog and Magog Division's financial results, or the copy of the lease on the Hushpucketie Plant or whatever you said you would do while in his or her office. In each letter either thank the buyer for taking the time to see you or mention that you are very much looking forward to your next meeting. Politeness is the best publicity you can generate.

GENERATING POSITIVE PUBLICITY REVIEWS

Positive Product Reviews in Trade Journals

Third-party endorsement can put people in seats for Broadway plays and movies better than any other form of promotion. A good reviewer like Clive Barnes, the New York ballet and theater critic, can generate major cash flow at the box office. A bad review from Mr. Barnes or others of his ilk can darken a theater in a fortnight.

Certain other products and services are affected by third-party endorsement or criticism. *Consumer Reports* can favorably or negatively impact a consumer appliance. Personal computer software relies for its initial lift-off on positive reviews in trade journals. In the early 1980s, dozens of new personal computer software companies were formed, each with bucketsful of venture capital, and many of which bought hundreds of pages of advertising to announce their capabilities. *Byte* magazine, the principal beneficiary of the rush of advertising, swelled to over 650 pages per issue, or almost as many pages as *Bride* magazine's June issue.

Alas, the advertising did nothing for the products but waste precious venture capital and cost the planet some trees. Ads do not give third-party endorsement. Reviews do. Ads identify the existence, availability, size, shape, color, and price of a product, but it takes a review to say, "Wow! This gizmo really works!"

Polling Positive Reviews

Short of creating one's own national association to endorse your product and service, and to gainsay all competitive products and services including those yet born, it is necessary to generate positive reviews. How is this done in an honest manner? I say "honest" because once a month we learn that automakers provide the reporters at certain automobile magazines with free cars or that a well-known pharmaceutical company pays esteemed physicians to rave about its drug. This seamy behavior is immoral and takes the fun out of closing deals.

My method for obtaining product reviews is to give the reporter a hook or a handle into a story that his or her readers would probably like to hear about. I think of reporters as if in a Shel Silverstein surrealist drawing, having two huge ears the size of normal bodies, sitting atop a tiny body the size of a normal ear. They live on information, hence their big ears that sit atop their heads like Scientific-Atlanta antennae. Mr. Silverstein, you may remember, drew the well-known ink-and-wash sketch of New York City for a *New Yorker* cover, where Manhattan Island occupies nine tenths of the country.

If you have a tasty tidbit for a trade journal reporter that relates to the features of the new product or service that you are trying to finance, then call or FAX it in to the reporter.

You cannot give the story to too many reporters at the same time however, because they like to be *sui generis* and not one of many on the receiving end of your scoop.

Performance Is the Best Endorsement

When planning your publicity campaign, remember two things. First, if your deal fails to happen, the publicity will backfire. If this happens, keep it to yourself.

Second, do not wait until you are in the middle of a deal to call on the trade press. Some magazine articles are written 60 to 90 days before we see them on the newsstands. Get started early on your publicity campaign.

PART TWO

TOOLS OF THE TRADE: DEAL-CLOSING AXIOMS

Winners generally set themselves apart from worthy competitors by how well they execute fundamentals. The same is true in closings as it is in sports.

There are six axioms or fundamentals in the closing process:

1. Understate your capabilities because overstating leads to disappointments.

2. Closings are enhanced when more people stand to benefit.

3. Fish with big hooks because they involve more disciples.

4. You can persuade people to do just about anything if you reward them with substantially more than their personal estimate of their own worth.

5. It's not so much what you've got, it's not even who you know. But what really counts is what you've got on who you know.

6. ILLEGITIMATI NON CARBORUNDUM EST. It means: Don't let the bastards wear you down.

Axiom 1: Understate Your Capabilities

The great deal-makers and poker players never expose all their cards upfront. They hold back some of the strongest points in their bag and wait until they learn more about what is on the buyer's mind. This is called *sand bagging* or *decoying*, and it originates in military usage.

Perhaps the greatest book of military strategy of all time is *The Art of War*, by Sun Tzu.* Written in 500 B.C., its strategies have been followed in war by Mao, Che Guevarra, Robert E. Lee, Stonewall Jackson, and Norman Schwarzkopf. If one treats deal-making as a military battle, as we will do when we consider deal-making in litigation and in bankruptcy negotiations, Sun Tzu should be studied in detail. But to underscore Axiom 1, let's listen to the words of the most heralded military strategist:

---

* Sun Tzu, *The Art of War*, translated by Samuel B. Griffith, Oxford University Press, London, 1963. Reprinted here by permission of Oxford University Press.

Pretend inferiority and encourage [the opposing commander's] arrogance.

If you overstate your capabilities, you are setting yourself up for failure. You can only fall short of them. You cannot exceed that which you have overstated. But if you understate your capabilities, or in Sun Tzu's words, if you "feign your capacities," you can exceed them, but it would be difficult to fall short.

Axiom 2: Benefit Lots of People

Closings are enhanced when more people stand to benefit. The more credit you can pass to others while maintaining the cash flow or the core assets of the deal, the more cheerleaders you will have pushing the deal toward a closing.

The day of the lone-wolf deal-maker is over. It takes networking, pulling together of disparate elements, persuading people to open important doors and make telephone calls to gatekeepers in order to close deals.

Axiom 3: Fish with Big Hooks

Small deals require as much time and energy to put together as do big deals. Small deals do not attract as many potential buyers. Small deals do not interest as many sponsors and cheerleaders.

The bigger the deal, the larger its impact. The bigger the fish you try to catch, the larger the hook you will need, the more hookmakers and the greater the feast when the fish is landed.

Deals concerning property began with the invention of the stirrup in the fifteenth century. The stirrup enabled men to wear armor on horseback. Men who could afford armor became formidable tanks, and they subdued men who fought on foot. The small farmer could not afford armor; he thus became either a serf or a craftsman who made armor in the employ of a lord who captured his land. The result of the discovery of the stirrup was a change in the landholding pattern and the control of wealth for centuries to come.

Axiom 4: Enhance the Buyer's Self-Image

Persuading a buyer to commit to your deal when he or she had no intention of doing your deal at the time you walked into the room is the art of deal-making. There must be something in the deal for the buyer that enhances his or her self-image.

The deal must make the buyer feel that he or she is part of a bigger world. It must project the buyer into a space greater than that which he or she currently occupies.

Axiom 5: It's Not Who You Know, It's What You Know About Them

There are rolodexes and there are Golden Rolodexes. The latter contain the names, addresses, telephone and FAX numbers, and *criteria for writing checks* of hundreds of buyers of deals. If you are going to wade into the deep and unknown waters of raising money to finance a deal, you will need to find people with Golden Rolodexes, and then interview them to determine if they know buyers for your specific deal.

These people are *finders*—the title that I give to what I do most of my waking hours. For professional reasons, the word finder is usually upgraded to investment banker, broker, dealer, or agent. There is a fee for the service of finding people to put money, assets, or other consideration into deals, and it ranges from 2 percent of the money raised, for large and not terribly difficult deals like finding a lender using hard and liquid collateral, to 50 percent for art dealers who use their walls and advertising money to attempt to sell the work of artists whose rolodexes are thin or nonexistent.

Experienced finders not only know who to go to with specific deals, they know quite a lot about the idiosyncrasies of the buyers, what they have made money in, what they have lost money in, their golf handicap, and favorite team. I have helped buyers find therapists, solve marital problems, improve their putting, and find discount vacation packages in many instances. Doing those kinds of favors makes my rolodex glitter.

Axiom 6: Don't Let Them Wear You Down

Illegitimati Non Carborundom Est is a Latin phrase that President Eisenhower kept on his desk in the White House. It means "Don't let the bastard wear you down."

You are going to get turned down a lot. Use the turndowns as springboards to push you to make more calls. Ask the buyer who turned your deal down for his or her reasons. Try to turn the turndown around by solving that buyer's particular needs.

There is a period of "pain" you go through in giving birth to a deal. There is a period of darkness when it appears that nobody will buy your deal. But these moments are necessary to strengthen you and teach you resilience. If deals were to come easy, everyone would do them. But they are not. They require some suffering. Nietszche said it best: "It takes a chaos to create a shooting star."

CHAPTER 7

POKER PLAYING: HOW TO DOWNPLAY YOUR CAPABILITIES

"Whether he likes it or not, a person's character is stripped bare at the poker table. If the other players perceive him as better than he really is, he has only himself to blame for subsequent losses. Unless he is both able and prepared to see himself as others do, flaws and all, he will be a loser in cards as in life." This quote is taken from of *Big Deal,*[*] written by poker player Anthony Holden.

Holden explains the art of bluffing in the book: "Misplaying hands deliberately can at times be a higher art form than playing to win," he writes.

Holden recommends looking like an idiot upfront in order to get the other players to bet into you wildly when you have a full house later on. This is a good strategy in poker playing. How does it transfer to business?

THE "BRAG TRAP": HOW APPEARING WEAK CAN GIVE YOU A COMPETITIVE EDGE

Appear in need of assistance to your prospective lenders. Ask for their involvement and participation. This appeals to the new banking

---

[*] Holden, Anthony, *Big Deal,* Penguin Group, New York, 1990. Reprinted here with permission.

strategy: *relationship banking*. It makes a banker feel important to believe that you want his or her advice as well as the bank's money.

Appear weak to your competitors. Give them the feeling of your fragility and they will not waste time attacking you. Business is war and one of the greatest authorities on military strategies, Sun Tzu, wrote 2,000 years ago:

> "All warfare is based on deception. A skilled general must be master of the complementary arts of simulation and dissimulation; while creating shapes to confuse and delude the enemy he conceals his true dispositions and ultimate intent. When capable he feigns incapacity; when near he makes it appear that he is far away; when far away that he is near."[*]

Entrepreneurs who appear competent and who surround themselves with well-known captains of industry and science and who talk about how they are going to take over a marketplace in the business press raise the hackles of the competition, who immediately take steps to wipe them out. DeLorean Motor Company fell into the "brag trap" and it failed. Many biotech start-ups that tried to score home runs with big-name scientists and who talked about their potential break-through products were failed ventures five years later.

The Bird from Chicago

There was once a bird who lived in Chicago who thought he was smarter than all the other birds.

"I'll not fly South this winter," he said. "It's too much trouble. I'll stay in Chicago and find a way to stay warm. I'm smart enough to do that."

So, as autumn turned to winter, and the temperature dropped, all the birds in Chicago began to fly South, except for the "smart" bird. He stayed behind.

---

[*] Sun Tzu, *The Art of War,* introductions by Samuel B. Griffin, Oxford University Press, London, 1963, p. 41. Reprinted here by permission of Oxford University Press.

But, when the snows came and the icy winds howled, even the "smart" bird could take it no longer.

"I must fly South," he said.

He took off in a storm, and things went well for awhile. The flapping of his wings kept the Chicago bird warm enough to fly at a pretty good speed through the snowflakes.

"I'm flying pretty fast," said the bird to no one in particular.

Just as he began to feel that he was out of the danger point, ice began to form under the bird's wings and he soon fell out of the sky to his certain death.

The Chicago bird dropped with a splat, straight into a fresh warm cow patty.

The cow patty saved him from certain death. "I'm alive," the bird said.

"I'm not only smart," said the bird in a loud, proud voice, "I'm lucky." And he started to get comfortable in the cow patty while the storm passed through.

Several hours later, the bird became hungry. Fortunately, there was enough grass and straw in the cow patty that the bird could survive on it for several days while he built up his strength to continue South.

The bird was so thrilled with his good fortune that he began to sing.

A cat heard the bird singing and came and ate him.

The moral of this story is that if you talk about how smart you are, you may have a crash landing. You may survive the crash landing, but have to eat a little dung to live through it and make a recovery. If you have to eat dung, don't talk about it.

FEDERAL EXPRESS AND THE ELEGANT BLUFF

The air freight companies and commercial airlines that carry cargo for freight forwarders permitted Federal Express to gain a significant chunk of their market before responding, mainly because they thought Fred Smith's concept was too simplistic. Emery's CEO, John Emery, called Federal's fleet of airplanes "Smith's expensive toys."

As Federal Express grew larger, it attracted more and more attention through advertising and hirings and took customers from UPS, Airborne Freight, and Emery. The company began to fight back in the period from 1977 to 1982 and threw all the force—political, financial and economic—that it could muster at the small company.

"The UPS decision to operate an overnight air service [in 1982] was considered the greatest challenge Federal Express had ever received."[*]

Fred Smith and his band of innovative managers responded to UPS with an elegant bluff, as Sigafoos explains.[**]

"UPS began its new service in September 1982. Its delivery commitment was by 3:00 P.M. the next day in its initial 24-city market network. It offered no 'on-call' pickup service and no tracing service on packages from the point of pickup to delivery. A customer's packages had to be ready to go at the time UPS drivers made their scheduled daily calls to the vicinity of the customer's office, plant, or warehouse. When Fred Smith heard of this he announced publicly, 'If you're using UPS and you miss the afternoon pickup, it's too bad. The last stage has left Dodge. There's the "Get Mad Factor" for UPS to worry about if the shipper has no alternative left to him.'

"At a meeting of Chicago security analysts held in the Palmer House during October 1982, Smith was quizzed hard about the competitive threat of UPS. He responded bluntly, 'Look, the 21 Club in New York and McDonald's are in the same business, but *there is a great deal of difference*.' Federal's counterattack was based on differentiating the quality of service. His public relations staff sent out this message: 'UPS is the best in the business at what they do —moving low priority, consumer-oriented parcels where emergency is not a factor. But Federal, in turn, is best at what it does—movement of the most vital and time-sensitive parcels and documents.'[***]

---

[*] Sigafoos, Robert A., *Absolutely Positively Overnight*, New American Library, New York, 1983, p. 155.

[**]Op.cit., pp. 157–158.

[***]Op.cit., p.181.

"Federal's marketing goal for 1983 was to establish clearly in the minds of customers that it offered a superior service.

"Explained Tom Oliver, head of marketing, 'We wanted to dispel in the minds of the customers the idea that competitors are the equal to us when in fact they are not. We're not going to let competitors equal Federal Express. We will offer 10:30 A.M. delivery, more service options, Saturday pickups, package tracing, and call-backs to shippers informing them that the packages have been delivered.'

"In the 1980s, the small-package market started to be quite crowded. New firms entered, and several existing firms like Emery, Airborne, Purolator Courier, and the leading commercial airlines stepped up their marketing efforts. Federal Express had defined the market and established its beachheads and gained control of strategic market areas in the preceding years, and consequently they woke up to the fact that there was a huge market out there for small packages and documents needing some form of priority service.

"An all-out media battle commenced among the principal competitors to convince the customer that each company could provide a fast, more reliable service. Federal's original priority commitment had been to deliver before 12:00 noon the next business day. Then, disregarding the enormous initial additional costs of the decision in October 1982 in response to mounting competition—particularly from UPS—Federal advanced its overnight service commitment to 10:30 A.M. At that time, Emery and Airborne offered a 'by 12:00 noon at the latest' service. Some of Federal's competitors offered a late afternoon service at a substantially lower price for those customers not caring whether their packages came in the morning or the afternoon. And most companies, including Federal, offered a second-day service at even lower prices.

"When the company acquired its fleet of 727s and DC-10s, built its Super Hub in Memphis, installed its state-of-the-art electronic communication system, and added other support facilities, Willmott proudly announced, 'We've got the best service; we've got the capacity; we've got the talent; we've got the best team; we're ready and open for business.' What Smith and Willmott were telling their competitors in so many words was, 'If anyone tries to get Federal Express, we'll get them first.'"

Clearly, the alligators at Federal Express had lured the Emery and UPS bears into the capital intensive, high-tech swamp and would try to keep them occupied while Federal captured the high ground.

Tiny Federal Express was showing a pair of threes face up to the other players, but betting and kicking the bets up and forcing the other players to pay much money to stay in the game and draw better cards. Federal Express did not have the resources to deliver on its promise of 10:30, but attempting to fulfill that promise was a superior alternative to going head to head with $5 billion (revenues) UPS for the same service—afternoon delivery. Federal Express said, in effect, "We're different and we're better." UPS and the other competitors were bluffed into staying in the game and have tried, less successfully, to capture market share over the last nine years.

WHY INVENTORS FREQUENTLY LOSE

The paranoia of inventors of patented products is the direct result of their absence of closing skills. Inventors frequently complain that their innovative products are licensed to major manufacturing companies that do nothing with them. They receive a small payment, but no royalties over time because the licensee never markets the product. It just sits there. Many inventors see the uniqueness of their product, but no more than that.

The licensee is a *gatekeeper* that controls a market or market segment. When it spots innovation that could capture some of its market share, it spends some money to block out the intruder. This frequently takes the form of locking up the marketing rights to newly-patented products, but then sitting on them.

How do large corporations hear about innovation in the first place? Via reading about patents in the Congressional Record or elsewhere. *Filing a patent makes you appear to be a* Wunderkind. The inventor who files a patent in order to get it issued is like the Chicago bird. That's because patents must be publicized.

Patent pendings do not have to be made public. Smart inventors know to raise their venture capital and establish their marketing agreements *before* getting a patent issued in order to keep their innovations quiet and out of the limelight. The *date of conception* protects the invention's inherent value and not the date of issuance.

Lawyers frequently advise inventors to file for a patent and to get it issued in order to protect the inventor's idea. Nothing could be further from the truth. This is bad advice. But it increases legal fees. Lawyers also recommend that troubled companies file for protection under Chapter 11 of the Federal Bankruptcy Act. This is also bad advice. But it generates legal fees. The opposite of legal advice is frequently the right thing to do in business: Do not do anything that requires a public filing if it can be avoided. Invisibility is a friend because it keeps the competition poorly informed and in the dark. And if your competition does not know that it is competing with you, it cannot defend itself from you, and you have a tremendous advantage over it by virtue of your silence and absence of publicity. It is not unlike playing poker skillfully.

TELL PEOPLE YOU ARE BREAKING ABOUT EVEN

To foil the competition, you know not to talk about how smart you are; you know that it is important to keep your head under the hood; and you know not to make a public filing or to bring public attention to your innovation or your plans if it can be avoided. Feign incapacity when you have strength, advises Sun Tzu. Operate in the shadows when you are outnumbered.

This is wisdom, but not necessarily practical advice. When the reporter from the leading trade journal is holding on the telephone for you to confirm or deny a rumor, what do you do? You can't refuse all requests for information, yet you do not want to overdo it like the Chicago bird. The answer lies in middle ground; that is, on the one hand things look great, but on the other hand they could get lousy pretty quick. Tell the reporter that there is as much to be enthusiastic about as there is to be negative. In other words, you're pretty much breaking even.

This is advice from the great poker players who live and die on the nuance and inflection of their opponents' comments and their opponents' reactions to their comments. Anthony Holden warns us about the competitions' remarks:

> But beware, above all, of the man who simply tells you he broke even. *He* is the big winner.*

The character Shelly in the Pulitzer Prize winning play *Steel Magnolias* says much the same thing: "Daddy always says 'An ounce of pretension is worth a pound of manure.'"

PEOPLE PLEASERS MAKE POOR DEAL-MAKERS

Some people should never go into business on their own. They have a carload of emotional pathologies that will cause them to fail. Chief among these is the *pleaser*.

The pleaser is a person who says "yes" to everything, and rarely says "no" or asks "why." When the bank asks for a personal guarantee, the pleaser goes along with it to please the banker. When the supplier says it is going to raise the prices of raw materials and it wants to collect payment in 30 rather than 45 days, the pleaser goes along with it. When the employee says he or she cannot work the necessary hours previously agreed to because of new developments yet wants to keep the job, the pleaser goes along with it and tosses in a small raise to show he or she really wants to please.

According to John Bradshaw, a leading family therapist, the pleaser is a person whose development was arrested in the area of parental recognition and rewards. The pleaser's parents ignored his or her childhood accomplishments, and the adult pleaser has a child within still seeking parental acclamation. The pleaser's parents were frequently workaholics or alcoholics or otherwise too busy and detached to be attentive to the overachieving child. The consequence to the child

---

* Holden, pp. 63–64.

is a low level of self-esteem and a high level of guilt in not being perfect in all aspects of his life. Bradshaw's pleaser is toxically guilty and has the following characteristics:

CHARACTERISTICS OF TOXIC GUILT[*]

Responsibility and Power:	Grandiose responsibility; way to be powerful in a powerless system.
Felt Sense:	Somber-serious; no place for mistakes. I can't make a mistake—it would be terrible.
Fault:	Belief that you are responsible for other's life.
Morality Goodness:	I can be good if I'm perfect.
Boundary:	I have no right to a boundary.

The pleaser is a poor deal-maker. He or she assumes far too much responsibility, strives for perfection instead of satisfaction, attempts to gain power through business victories, and allows too many people to know far too much about his or her business. Rather than maintaining invisibility, he or she talks too much. Rather than telling the banker who asks the pleaser for his or her personal guarantee in order to make a loan—"If you need my guarantee, you shouldn't be making this loan"—the pleaser signs on the dotted line and puts his or her personal assets at risk. Rather than delegating responsibility throughout the organization, the pleaser takes on more and more because he or she feels that it is imperative to achieve perfection, to operate without mistakes, and that only he or she is fully capable of doing things right.

---

[*] Bradshaw, John, *Healing The Shame That Binds You*, Health Communications, Inc., Deerfield Beach, Florida, 1988.

BLUFFING AND SAYING NO

If the purpose of business is to make your product or service substitutes for those of all competitors and to make their products and services no substitutes for yours, then when you are small and innovative and your competitors are large, established, and conservative, the dual strategies of the *bluff* and the *no* are critical to closing deals. They frequently go hand in hand.

For example, I was at one point negotiating the purchase of a $20 million (sales) distribution company. Its earnings before interest and taxes (EBIT) or cash flow was $1,750,000, and its net worth was $5,900,000. I offered $5,100,000, of which $4,100,000 would be cash at closing (leveraged on the company's assets), and $1,000,000 was an earn-out and seller's note, divided roughly in half.

The sellers were being asked to remain with the company as management, and to bind them to the company I conceived a back-end payment plus an added bonus for delivering bottom-line results. The sellers asked me to guarantee the $1,000,000 back-end payment personally.

I said no. The reason for not paying 100 percent cash at closing, I argued, was that I needed to "incentivize"them positively to work as hard for the new owner as they did for themselves. "You should guarantee *me* that you will perform," I countered. I was bluffing. I knew they would work just as hard for me as they did for themselves because work was the most important thing in their lives. Plus, they wanted the $1,000,000 back-end payment, and they had to produce the cash flow to make it happen.

They remained steadfast in their demand for a personal guarantee. I put my feet in cement and said no. I argued that I must have them "at risk" in order to assure myself that they would work just as hard for the new owner. I would have given them limited or partial personal guarantees to save the deal, but they believed that I wouldn't budge from my no.

We were at an impasse, but they did not say "This is a deal breaker," so I knew they were ready to cave in. I added another reason, nonverifiable but enticing—a second bluff.

"We're going to buy other companies using your company as the base," I offered. "If I give you a personal guarantee, it will appear in the footnotes to the financial statements, and future sellers will see it and demand it. I can't keep giving it out because it will become worthless. I'm not that rich."

The second bluff worked. The sellers accepted the $1,000,000 back-end payment fully at risk without my personal guarantee. My logic was simplistic and naive. I gave the reasons one at a time, and not as a bill of particulars. I left myself plenty of maneuvering room, particularly in the price, so that I could have traded a little more on price if they had asked for it. But, they accepted the simplistic logic that (1) I needed them to prove to me that they could deliver the cash flow to make their back end payments happen; and (2) my personal guarantee would be asked for again in the future if it appeared in the footnotes, and soon it would be worthless.

WEIGHT WATCHERS PROPOSITION

When Jean Nidetch started Weight Watchers International in the mid-1960s, the premise of her business plan was as follows:

> I will rent a motel conference room and announce via inexpensive newspaper ads that overweight people are invited to come to the conference room and pay my company $2 for the privilege of standing up in front of everyone and saying why they are fat and what they intend to do about it. After everyone has spoken, the conference will end, and I will sell products to the people as they leave such as books, tapes, menus and, when I raise more capital, low-calorie food and dressings.

The proposition is simplicity itself. The customers loved it. They bought the deal, and Weight Watchers prospered and was soon acquired by H. J. Heinz for $91 million. Giant food processing corporations that should have dominated the diet food and wellness-products market ignored Weight Watchers International and the other wellness start-ups because their solution-delivery systems appeared too simplistic. In fact, they are brilliant and as time-tested as the Bible.

8

Enticing People with Benefits

Samuel Goldwyn, the highly successful and oft-quoted movie mogul known for, among other things, the famous dance numbers with the "Goldwyn Girls" in the movies of the 1930s and 1940s, was once shooting a Biblical movie with large crowd scenes. Goldwyn's instincts told him that the public wanted to see crowds of people and syncopated movements by collections of people, something like the "wave" that fans do at football games. For a certain scene that Goldwyn was shooting involving Jesus, he asked his assistant for more disciples.

The assistant said, "Mr. Goldwyn, Jesus had only twelve disciples."

"What do you mean only twelve disciples?" demanded Goldwyn. "I want thousands."

The more people who are on the screen doing something in relation to someone else, the greater the harmonic modulation, Goldwyn believed, and notwithstanding the story line, the audience had to appreciate the technique. If the story is the *relationship*, then the technique is the *transaction*. We see this in "chase scene" movies such as *Star Wars* and *Dances with Wolves*, which inevitably do well at the box office for myriad reasons not the least of which is the involvement of thousands of "disciples."

Deal-closers borrow a page from Goldwyn's play book. Sam Walton involved hundreds of city and county officials, created thousands of jobs, and promised lower prices to millions of people in order to raise hundreds of millions of dollars in loans to finance his Wal-Mart stores. Ross Perot paid visits to dozens of his employees' spouses with stock certificates in their names to buy their loyalty in exchange for not seeing their husbands for months on end as Perot sent them off on software installation contracts. Sol Price sold thousands of memberships to his Price Clubs to finance the building of warehouse-sized stores and the purchase of inventory. These megabuck closers knew that if they involved many people in the success of their deal, if they disbursed the credit for success, they would win big.

Thus the second axiom of deal-closers:

Closings are enhanced when more people stand to benefit.

YELTSIN GOES DOWN BETTER THAN GORBACHEV

Maximilian Robespierre, a leader in the French Revolution, 1793–1794, clearly stated the ideal that gave fuel to the revolution. The strictness with which he held to his ideal—that moral virtue was inseparable from sovereignty—won him the approval of the French people. But once the revolution got into full flower and the peasants demanded their full share of freedom, Robespierre's staunch position prevented his becoming a "man of the people," and he was guillotined by the Counter-Revolutionists. What he set in motion got away from him, and Robespierre missed the revolutionary train.

Mikhail Gorbachev set the Russian Revolution of 1991 in motion five years ago with his calls for *perestroika* and *glasnost*. But during the coup of August 1991, it was Boris Yeltsin who took control of the revolution when he climbed to the top of the Soviet tank and spoke to millions of people.

This history lesson may not appear to have much to do with deal-making, but don't put your head in the sand. You may explicate the benefits and attributes of your deal better than any spokesperson has ever done in the past or may so do in the future. But lacking the support of the people who stand to benefit from your deal, you may end up on the bottom of the pile, like Robespierre, while the parade marches on.

FRANCHISING

Few business strategies ever conjured by the innovative minds of capitalists work as well as *franchising*. Retail commercial establishments such as fast-food restaurants that do not require sophisticated management at the point of sale are frequently developed as franchisees. For a one-time fee plus a monthly royalty (typically 5 percent of the retailers' sales), a retailer buys the right to operate a small business whose product is advertised nationally. He or she is equipped with an operating manual, training, national advertising, referrals through an 800 number, a recognizable logo, and an annual franchisees' meeting to exchange information and ideas.

One of the reasons franchising works so well is that so many people are involved in friendly competition. Monthly bulletins published by the franshisor on behalf of franchisees rank the top producers and reward them with visible praise of their fellow franchisees. The winners are given special awards, such as gold bolo tie clasp replicas of Colonel Sanders with diamond insets, wall plaques, and vacations to Hawaii or the Caribbean.

But the greatest reward of all is for a franchisee to be acquired by the parent company for a cigar box full of stock certificates sufficient to reward her with wealth for her achievements. In fact, if franchisors do not acquire their most successful franchisees, the game loses much of its incentive and the glue that holds the franchisees together becomes watery and no longer binds the players together.

Attending a franchisees' annual meeting is the equivalent of participating in an evangelists' tent meeting. The message is essentially the same: pull together, seed the faith, work harder so that others may receive the blessings that we have found. There are images indelibly engraved on my brain from having attended many of each of these kinds of meetings. The message of tent and franchisee meetings is the same: Seed the faith ye faithful so that our mission can be brought to those who have not yet seen the light. In business jargon this means buy into the deal and together with others of like mind we will sell our message to the multitudes.

THE TOWN MEETING

Another time-honored tradition that is often appropriated in closing deals is the *town meeting*. If your deal involves launching, saving, or acquiring a local business, there is no more persuasive oil for the gears of local commerce than the promise of jobs. Increased employment in a community benefits everyone, from pharmacist to schoolteacher, from mayor to cosmetologist.

Gaining community support requires involving community leaders in the deal and asking them for their ideas, contacts, contributions, and networking skills to make the deal happen. Pass the credit around. Appear as one among many. Let the politicians get credit for increased jobs, in consideration for the city's loan guarantees or the purchase of the company's bonds by government employee pension funds. Place insurance, and buy components and services locally. Hire graduates of the local community college. Spread the wealth while spreading the credit.

9

Fishing with a Big Hook: How to Spread the Wealth and Improve Your Chances for Success

Deal-makers know that they can involve more people if their proposition is big rather than small. If you are in the process of formulating plans to launch your deal, pause for a moment and examine the big picture. How many lives will your proposal positively affect? How many people will it enrich? How many jobs will be created? How many politicians can be given credit for its success? Spread the wealth and you will attract disciples and the disciples, will push the buyers to close the deal for you.

Which brings us to the third axiom of closings:

Fish with big hooks because they involve more disciples.

An esteemed Hungarian-born chemist named Albert Szent-Györgyi discovered the roles played by certain organic compounds including Vitamin C. He escaped political oppression in the late 1930s and came to the United States, where he continued his scientific research at Woods Hole, Massachusetts. As a diversion from a 14-hour workday, Szent-Györgyi took up fishing.

"I always fished with a big hook," said Szent-Györgyi to an audience of his peers at the end of his illustrious career.

"I knew I wouldn't catch anything. But it's more exciting to have a big one get away than to lose a small one."*

If you are an independent movie producer, an inventor at the workbench of innovation, or an entrepreneur attempting to launch a new service company, never forget that some states and certain counties within states will provide inexpensive loans and grants if you do your deal in their region and employ their citizens. The Bureau of Indian Affairs provides up to 100 percent financing if Native Americans are hired as movie extras, production workers, hotel employees, or in other productive capacities. Certain communities, particularly those in the rust belt, will provide financing on a ratio of $10,000 per new job that your business plan or projections estimate you will create. If your plan projects 40 new jobs, the states of Ohio, Pennsylvania, Illinois, Connecticut, and certain others have low interest-rate loans for you of as much as $400,000.

THE MULTIPLIER EFFECT OF BIG DEALS

Doing deals takes an incalculable amount of balancing of critical variables, players, and judgment. From start to finish, a deal might take anywhere from 60 to 180 days. In fact, if a deal does not close by then, you have made a mistake somewhere. If you are going to invest a considerable amount of time, money, and energy, why not shoot for the moon and do a big deal? Why not do a deal that changes the lives of many people for the better? That leaves definitive tracks in the sand of time. Indeed, why not?

Big deals, as opposed to small and niche-market deals, affect many people through a chain reaction of events, the net result of which is multiple cash flow channels for the deal-maker. To show you what I mean, let's look at the story of the world's *first deal-maker.*

---

* Szent-Györgyi, Albert, *Some Misplaced Ideas on Democracy,* Jeffrey Norton Publishers, Inc., Audio-Forum, Inc., Guilford, CT, 1990 (audio cassette).

The First Deal-Maker

Far back among the mists of time, a family prepared a feast for some important visitors from another tribe. In doing so, they created productivity, employment, and innovation.

The family hunted and killed many birds, harvested vegetables, and picked fruit and coconuts to feed their guests. They persuaded a friend to cut down a tree to build them a table and benches for the guests' comfort. They asked others to clear an area from the jungle in which the feast could be held. Still others were asked to cook, serve, and clear away the meal. All told, a dozen people worked on the feast, and the family promised each of them a reward when the feast was over.

The feast was lavish and beautifully prepared. It tasted better than any meal the visitors had ever eaten. They promised to reciprocate, and a week later they sent the host family a fine goat as a thank-you present. The family gave goat's milk to all the people who helped them prepare the feast. The workers were so pleased with the way the law of reciprocity worked that they eagerly volunteered to help prepare another feast, and another, and another.

As the feast business flourished and was transformed into a large-scale restaurant operation, however, some of the workers grew bored with performing the same tasks day after day. One of them, the table maker, left the first entrepreneur's team and built himself a floating table, which he called a boat. He planned to purchase food from the feast-giver, load it into his boat, transport it to nearby islands, and sell it to the tribes who lived there. The family of restaurant owners saw this enterprise as a second source of revenue, so they invested in the food exporting business.

Life is random, however, and rewards are uncertain. When the exporter arrived on the nearby island with his cargo of food, the tribe welcomed him with cries of joy and offered him a thousand coconuts as his reward. But it was not the food that they wanted, for they had plenty of that; it was his boat.

They explained to him that their island was heavily populated, a situation that had created a tremendous waste-removal problem. If the visitor would make boats for them, they would easily be able to cart their waste away.

Like many a deal-maker in the centuries to follow, this food exporter found that he had to make a major change in his plans. There was no food shortage problem for him to solve, so he had to give up the export business. There was, however, a serious need for boats. Because all good deal makers are flexible, the food exporter quickly transformed himself into a boat manufacturer. Also, this deal maker had learned management skills by working for the restaurant. He had, in other words, all the components of the formula: a large problem, a good solution, and an excellent management team—himself and the workers he trained.

One of the boat maker's cleverest workers achieved a high-technology breakthrough: He invented the wheel. He decided to use his invention to solve the widespread problem of waste removal. To that end he and his family began to produce wheelbarrows, which could be used to cart waste to the shore where the second deal-maker's boats waited. After firmly establishing his wheelbarrow business, he took advantage of many other entrepreneurial opportunities by setting up a waste-hauling enterprise, a wheel-manufacturing business, and dozens of other operations that relied on the wheel.

As years passed, many other enterprises were spun off from the original three. The circle of problem solving kept widening to include more and more solutions and receivers of those solutions. Service organizations were established, and the manufacture of components became an important industry. The tribal people came to understand that their profits would exceed their costs by a significant margin as long as three circumstances prevailed:

1. The solutions had to solve large problems for the receivers.

2. The solutions had to be unique or presented in a unique, non-duplicable manner.

3. The law of reciprocity had to be obeyed to the letter.

Many inventor-entrepreneurs (like the one who invented the wheel) develop elegant solutions first, and then find suitable problems for them. Note that the formulation of a problem is crucial, however, for no matter how unique the solution may be, it is of little or no value if it is not needed to solve a serious problem. Contrary to Benjamin Franklin's claim, *people will not beat a path to your door if you develop a better mousetrap, for that is a solution which lacks a big problem.*

MULTIPLE CASH FLOW CHANNELS

Multiple cash flow channels exist for each of the three entrepreneurial companies in the story. Competent deal-makers are capable of multiplying their wealth by introducing new solutions and offering them to the established receivers via unique methods. For example, the family of restaurateurs could open additional restaurants on nearby islands, sell franchises to tribes on faraway islands, package their delicacies for sale at boat docks, launch a gourmet magazine, and publish their recipes. The boat manufacturer could start a rent-a-boat business or operate boats under contract for islands that prefer to have their transport needs managed by someone more experienced than themselves. The wheelbarrow manufacturer could establish a wheelbarrow rental agency, operate a garbage-removal business under contract for tribes who prefer that service, and exploit his wheel as a component part of other products.

There is a rule of thumb that for every job created by an entrepreneurial company one additional job is created in the community to service the employee and his or her family. These jobs are filled by teachers, beauticians, clerks, service station attendants, and the like.

Note the myriad services for which these first three deal-makers created a need. The restaurateur created a need for laundry, linen supply, printed menus, graphic art for signs and menus, garbage removal, fresh flowers for tables, furniture, music to create a familiar ambience, uniforms for the waiters and waitresses, and advertising and public relations to inform receivers about the service. With further expansion, the first deal-makers would require day-care services for their employees' children, lawyers to draft franchising agreements, and a marketing team to sell their delicacies at boat docks and to sell franchises to faraway tribes.

The services created by the second deal-maker, the boat-maker, include leasing consultants, travel agents to schedule trips for sales personnel, bankers to open letters of credit, and facilities management consultants to assist in pricing and operating the transportation management services to other islands.

The third deal-maker, the inventor, needs assistance in industrial design because his or her wheels, which are made of coconuts, have a tendency to crack when a heavy load is carted in the wheelbarrow. He or she also needs engineers, financial consultants, and management consultants. Inventors seem to require the greatest number of service professionals to fill the gaps in their knowledge.

Multiple Job Creation

Deal-makers, in other words, generate not only wealth but also jobs, many of which are in the community at large rather than inside the company headquarters. As new businesses are established, they create a need for myriad service employees in the adjacent area: accountants, lawyers, advertising and marketing people, maintenance crews, teachers, and health care personnel. Another development often occurs as innovative projects and companies are established: Local citizens receive an opportunity to invest in them. If a sufficient number of people in a community stand to benefit, the number of local cheerleaders multiplies.

THE LAUNCH OF CONTROL DATA CORPORATION

Few deals have raised as much start-up capital in their communities (and made as many local millionaires) as did Control Data Corporation. The germ of the idea for what would become one of the largest computer manufacturers in the world originated with William C. Norris. Norris had climbed up through the heavy organizational structure at Sperry Rand, when in 1955 he grew frustrated with excessive paperwork and an inhibiting senior management structure.

Norris was ripe for a change when Arnold Ryden, a financial consultant, Byron Smith, a UNIVAC executive, and Willis K. Drake, Norris's assistant (later the founder and Chief Executive Officer of Data Card Corporation), approached him in early 1957. They planted the seed in his mind to launch a new company—another ERA—free to grow without a corporate bureaucracy. Ryden wrote a business plan. Norris reached the end of his rope at Sperry and resigned. Drake became Control Data's first employee and it was his task to raise the initial capital. As it is described in *Self-Made:**

Sell stock, his collaborators said. It was an extraordinary idea. Never in history, the Minnesota securities commissioner told Drake, have the founders of a new company personally tried to sell their own stock.

Drake showed the commissioner the Control Data prospectus. Control Data's mission statement was thin. The company would engage in research and development of electronic equipment. Nothing was said about building computers. Furthermore, the company said it did not intend to compete directly with giants like IBM, Sperry Rand and General Electric.

The securities commissioner searched his rule books looking for some regulation that outlawed personal sale of new company stock by its founders. There was none. He handed Drake all the forms he needed and expected never to see him again.

"The idea that we could sell stock in a company with no product, no employees and no facility seemed totally preposterous to him," Drake recalls. Drake set about trying to sell the stock anyway. He drank countless cups of coffee at Mrs. Strandy's Coffee Shop in St. Paul with potential investors. He met others at the Parker House Restaurant in Mendota ("when people didn't want to be seen with me"). But the process was too slow. Drake invited a dozen people to his home instead.

"One engineer said he wanted 10,000 shares," Drake recalls. "Up to that time I had sold 500. The second night we had another meeting: this time 25 people showed up. The third night, there

---

* Carol Pine and Susan Mundale, *Self-Made* (Minneapolis, Minnesota: Dorn Books, 1982).

were cars parked for blocks up and down the street in every direction. People called from New York and California. The whole thing cascaded. Investors were buying the principals led by William Norris as much as they were buying the idea for a company.

One objective was to distribute Control Data stock as widely as possible. The future of this new venture, the cofounder decided, would not be vested in a single large shareholder like John Parker.

The stock sold easily—615,000 shares at $1 a share in less than two weeks. About 300 people, chiefly UNIVAC employees and personal friends of Control Data officers, invested. Norris himself bought 75,000 shares—having "mortgaged nearly everything to do that," according to a colleague. Then Norris and Ryden arranged a two-year note with First Bank of Minneapolis for the principal investors. The bank was willing to lend each man four times his investment, with his Control Data stock pledged as collateral. ("That," Bill Drake says, "was an enlightened bank.") Even Jane Norris, Bill Norris' wife, put in some of her own money for Control Data stock. "If we lose all of it," she said at the time, "we'll just move ourselves and our six children back to the farm in Nebraska."*

In attempting to build a strong, local board of directors, Norris visited the elder statesman of 3M Corporation and painted a vivid picture of Control Data's future. "Hell," the 70-year-old 3M chairman said, "if I were 20 years younger, I'd invest. And I'll tell you this, too, sonny: If I were UNIVAC, I'd sue." In fact, Sperry Rand sued Control Data, forcing Norris to sign a consent order. In the meantime, Control Data's stock rose from 33 cents to $11.25 per share. Norris began growing Control Data's revenues rapidly. He also saved money wherever he could.

Control Data staffers always told a manufacturer's representative selling electronic parts to arrive at 11:30 A.M., hoping he would buy them lunch. "I don't mind feeding the company," the representative said one day when he was asked to leave yet another armload of parts behind, "but I'll be damned if you're going to build your computer with my samples.

---

* Ibid, p. 112.

That computer was Seymour Cray's 1604—an instrument that would set Control Data's course for years to come and pull it out of its early poverty. Cray's 1604 meant that Control Data would not be the company described in the original mission statement. CDC would instead build a large-scale computer, and it would compete with the majors. The 1604 was compact, extremely versatile and, most important, priced at about half the cost of a competitive IBM computer. The 1604 was predicated on transistors, not vacuum tubes, and designed with complex printed circuit cards. "Printed building blocks," Cray called the cards. With those as a starting point, he theorized, a computer of almost any size could be built.

"No one else at Control Data would have thought of it," says Robert Kisch, a CDC engineer during that period. "No one else had the capability. The initial success of Control Data was due to Seymour Cray."

The 1604 had its debut eight months after Control Data was incorporated. Two months later, the company had its first order from the U.S. Navy Bureau of Ships. The $1.5 million sale to a "prestige customer" was crucial to the young company's credibility. About the same time, Norris, the man responsible for fund-raising, had also convinced Allstate Insurance to buy 350,000 shares of preferred stock at $25 per share. "We were rolling again on a full stomach," Norris recalls.

After the Navy order, new buyers of the 1604 fell into line, and Cray continued his imaginative tinkering. In 1959, Cray's Model 160 desk-sized computer selling for $90,000 enhanced the company's growing reputation for innovation. A year after that, Cray started work on the CDC 6600—bigger than IBM's "Stretch," until that time the largest computer ever built. The 6600 would cost $7 million per unit, and Norris offered a reporter the following understatement: "We won't have to make very many to make money..."

When Norris said in 1961, with similar understatement, "There are certain advantages to size," perhaps even he did not envision the momentum of that decade. After its first, unprofitable year, when total sales hovered around $780,000, CDC's figures were stunning: 1959, $4.5 million; 1960, $28 million; 1963, $100 million; 1965, $160 million; 1968, $841 million; 1969, $1 billion.

In 1961, only IBM, with a hammerlock on 82 percent of the computer market, and Control Data, with 1.6 percent of the market, were operating in the black. The computer divisions of Philco, Bendix, RCA, Packard-Bell and Honeywell all saw red ink. Norris' nemesis, Sperry Rand, was only just approaching profitability with its computers.*

---

* Ibid, p. 117.

CHAPTER 10

THE POWER OF PERSUASION

DONALD J. TRUMP AND TELEVANGELISTS: PUT YOUR FAITH—AND YOUR MONEY—IN MY HANDS

I am a Trumpwatcher and I am hooked on televangelists. Donald J. Trump's business plan is an elegant construction designed to make the buyer raise his or her own personal self-worth by millions of dollars. It is one thing to think you are a banker to whom people come daily and genuflect for money. It is quite another to be approached by the biggest builder since King Herod and persuaded that if you loan money to properties that bear the name "Trump" they will increase values and rates of return to your lending institution far greater than you ever dreamed because the name "Trump" is front-page news, thrills, romance, and adventure. You can be part of the magic. Sign the check and shoot it across the desk. Join the next great revolution.

Trump made a tragic error: he guaranteed about half of his loans personally. He didn't have to. His business plan was compelling enough. It is possible to borrow as much money without personal guarantees as it is by giving them. It simply takes some negotiating skill and time. Someone who continually gives his or her personal guarantee to obtain financing *needs* to give it in order to please the lender. Whereas saying "no" to the lender makes a "yes" of the borrower.

You can persuade people to do just about anything if you reward them with substantially more than their personal estimate of their own worth. This is the fourth axiom of the deal-closing process.

The Biblical Derivative of Consumer Service Companies

The deal that is struck between entrepreneurs and their franchisees is based on *trust*. It is as old as Judeo-Christian scripture and based on the Golden Rule: Do unto others as you would have them do unto you.

The entrepreneur says to the franchisee: "Send me your money in advance and I will give you territorial exclusivity, training manuals, advertising support, products, uniforms, and the privilege of joining with others like yourself at annual meetings where you will be whipped into a frenzy of enthusiasm for my fried chicken (or weight-loss program, or computer-portrait system, or muffler-repair service, or what have you)." The franchisee trusts the entrepreneur to deliver on his or her promise, signs a contract, and sends a check. The deal is struck.

The church for centuries has obtained its financial support by asking its communicants to pay a portion of their income in return for what it provided them. In the magnificent Renaissance-era church of the Gesuati in Venice hangs the *Crucifixion* by Tintoretto and the celebrated frescoed ceiling by G. B. Tiepolo of the *Institution of the Rosary*.

The Tiepolo ceiling has the Virgin in glory with the Child surrounded by clouds of angels. Below them is St. Dominic who, having driven out heresy, is distributing rosaries. In the mornings, deliverymen arrive with boxes and stack them in front of Tintoretto's Crucifixion. They contain candles that will be lighted and put into candelabras placed throughout the chapel by believers who will have paid 100 lire or more, depending on the candles' size, for the privilege of worshiping there.

Churches built in the late twentieth century cannot re-create the magnificent Gesuati or the Duomo in Milan because the capital does not exist. The founders of the new churches, whom we call televangelists, use the communications satellite to beam their messages of healing, prosperity, and power into the homes of their believers whose church is the television set. Rather than pay to light a candle underneath a Tintoretto, the subscribers to the messages of televangelists send $15 or more to "seed their faith." The deal is struck between the preacher and the believer, or the entrepreneur and the consumer, and it is done via a contract of faith and trust governed by the Law of Reciprocity that is as old as time itself.

Televangelism and the Contract of Faith

Nowhere is the contract of faith more explicit than in the televangelism market where self-proclaimed descendants of Jesus of Nazareth, such as Jim Bakker and his *Praise the Lord* television ministry. The premise of the deal is substantially the same in televangelism as it is in the proclamations of Donald J. Trump: *You are greater than you think.*

Televangelist to Christian Faithful	Donald J. Trump to His Banking Faithful
You are worth more than you are paid and if you send whatever amount of money you can to my ministry, more people like you will get to hear the word as you have heard the word and be healed and together we will change things so that your true worth will be recognized. I am here to help you should your faith ever weaken.	You are worth much more than they pay you, and if you loan money to my hotels and casinos, unbelievable riches will flow to your institution and you will be rewarded in kind. I am here to help you should your faith ever weaken.

Both Bakker and Trump outcompeted their mentors. Their products achieved the goal of business: *to make all competitive products no substitute for yours, while making your product a substitute for all others.*

Bakker resigned from his multimillion dollar television ministry in March 1987 when his sexual dalliance with former church secretary Jessica Hahn became public. He was later indicted for using his satellite television empire to pitch his viewers bogus lifetime annual vacations to Heritage USA, his sprawling 2,300-acre theme park in South Carolina financed with the $1,000 tithes of 141,000 evangelical Christians.

During the five-year run of Bakker's *Praise the Lord*, sometimes called "People Who Love" ministry, Bakker raised $158 million via direct appeals to his flock. Although much of the money was used for the ministry's daily operations, Bakker was convicted of diverting $3.7 million toward the purchase of vacation homes, a fleet of Rolls Royces and Mercedes, furs, Rolex watches, face lifts for himself and his wife, and an air-conditioned doghouse for their pet.

Jim Bakker and other televangelists altered the teachings of Jesus, isolated passages from the Bible to fit their needs—such as the all-purpose Isaiah 53:5: "By his wounds we are healed"—and reoriented the message of Christianity from a God-centered to a man-centered and from a holiness-centered to a happiness-centered focus. Bakker and his competitors offered power in an era of impotence, magic in a time of fear, divinity in a time of human weakness. "Name it and claim it," he said. "Mail your $15 to PTL and we will unlock heaven's storehouse of blessings for you."

The Jim and Tammy show was not the only televangelism deal that the nation's approximately 40 million evangelical Christians were offered in the 1980s. In 1985, according to Arbitron, the top 20 syndicated religious programs had more than 11 million viewers. Oral Roberts, who has conducted a healing ministry for 43 years, announced in 1987 that God would end his life if viewers did not contribute $4.5 million toward a medical missionary project. This cost him half of his 1.1 million viewers. Deal-makers know that this sell has no demonstrable economic proposition.

Jimmy Swaggart, who preached to 2.2 million viewers in 192 markets in November 1985, was defrocked by the Assemblies of God in 1988 for sexual improprieties and now speaks to 404,000 households in 77 markets. Pat Robertson, head of the Christian Broadcasting Network, who took time off to run for President of the United States in 1988, claims to have raised $80 million from his *700 Club* members who are asked to send in $20 per month to seed their faith.

A service sell *cannot* revert from its demonstrable economic proposition of, in this case: Seed your faith so that others may see the light; be healed or gain the power that this ministry has given you.

The Bakkers proposed a project, Heritage USA, and this chunk of Carolina real estate obfuscated their message. Oral Roberts switched his sell to "save my life," but the premise had no DEP factor. Pat Robertson made a run for the Presidency, which diverted his buyers.

To their credit, the televangelists who stuck to their message— Robert H. Schuller's *Hour of Power*, Reverend Billy Graham's Calvinist gospels, and Reverend Ken and Gloria Copeland's *Health and Wealth Gospel*—are prospering here and abroad because their premise is indefatigably consistent.

Trump's Business Plan— It's All in the Name

Trump persuaded commercial loan officers to allow him access to several billion of their depositors' dollars so that he might buy properties in order to put his name on them because—and here's the demonstrable economic proposition of Trump's business plan that the bankers actually *bought*—when properties bore the name *Trump*, customers would flock to them in droves because the image of power, wealth, and risk-taking would compel them to do so. How very televangelical the Trump message sounds, especially when you insert the word "Trump" for "God" in the following passage: "God's got it, I can have it, and by faith I'm going to get it."[*]

---

[*] Horton, Michael, *The Agony of Deceit*, Moody Press, Chicago, p. 50.

Trump understands that his purpose as a businessperson is to make his properties substitutes for all others while making competitive properties no substitutes for his. He competes in the extraordinarily belligerent fields of hospitality, gambling, and residential real estate in one of the most litigious regions of the country, the New York City metropolitan area. Sinatra has sung "If I can make it there, I'll make it anywhere." That's how tough this market is, and Trump is nothing if not a survivor.

The premise of Trump's business plan is, in essence, the following:

> My casinos will achieve cash flows far above the norm as will my hotels, rental properties, resorts and airline because they will all bear the name *Trump* which means power, wealth, and risk and my customers—the meek, the middle class, and the afraid—will flock to my properties in never-before-achieved numbers. So open your vaults ye bankers (who are ironically so like my customers) and permit me to overbuild, overpay, and generally overextend myself and ye shall be rewarded with interest, principle, and kinship to me.

As you know, hotels are limited by their number of rooms and by the prices hotels in the same immediate area charge for similar rooms and meals sold to occupants. The same reasoning applies to casinos—a limited number of people can play blackjack, shoot craps, and wager at roulette and pull slot machine handles in a 24-hour period. With airlines, the limiting factor is revenues per seat per mile flown; a similar constraint applies to rental properties. These studies are *free*. Any of Trump's banker-gatekeepers could have ordered a copy. But why bother? As one banker told *Barrons*: "You never lost your job for lending to Donald Trump; you probably got a promotion."

Studies show that to break even after debt service, the Trump Taj Mahal had to achieve revenues that were simply not possible. The Trump Plaza Hotel's projections were similarly not achievable. Nor were those of the Trump Shuttle. A securities analyst with Janney Montgomery Scott was fired by his bosses, allegedly on Trump's orders, for saying just this. Thus, going into the deal, *a priori*, the bankers knew they would not get paid by the Taj Mahal and the Plaza and the Shuttle unless Trump's premise was accurate; i.e. throw out the industry studies fellas, the name *Trump* will bring in more money than any casino or hotel has ever achieved. You have to admit, Donald Trump sculpted a compelling premise. It was extremely defensible and did best under fire. The more that powerful people attacked Trump for his having screwed them or sued them or tattooed them in deals, and the more that he withstood the attacks, the more powerful his image grew and the more convinced the bankers were that Trump might be right.

The Difference Between Trump and Bakker

Bakker persuaded thousands of people to do his deal, write him a check, loosen their purse and "Close your eyes and hold a bill over your head. Somebody will come by and take it from you."

Trump persuaded fewer than a dozen bankers to toss away their industry studies, throw caution to the wind and abjure their years of training in corporate finance, and overloan him in order to buy the baubles that the weak and the fearful most prize. The handful of bankers, once persuaded, convinced others until the syndicate grew to about fifty. Trump, of Brooklyn, like Jesus of Nazareth, built his empire through developing disciples.

What Trump and Bakker have in common is that their deals did not add value. Yet these two deal-makers captured the hearts, minds, and pocket-books of millions of people for half a decade. They shifted wealth from other pockets to their pockets. They were the consumate *Deal-Makers*.

Bakker and Trump aren't the first Diplomats of the Deal to vest in their parishioners the power of positive thinking to enrich themselves. The point is this: Astute lenders and investors, like the poor lost souls who flock to the televangelists' tents, *want to be with a winner.*

SAY *NO* TO REQUESTS FOR YOUR PERSONAL GUARANTEE

Don't even think about becoming a winning deal-maker if you are too anxious to please. If you say "yes" to requests for personal guarantees, higher costs, impossible delivery schedules, more territory, free after-sale support and all sorts of benefits that shrewd buyers ask for, you will at some point disappoint the buyer and lose the project, the company, the invention, the screenplay, the concept, or whatever it is you're trying to make a deal on.

Either take on a partner who does not have boundary problems and who does not have the need to achieve grandiose results by blanketing him- or herself in impossible layers of responsibility—that is, a partner who reflexively says "no" to every request that buyers make—or write the *Book of No's.*

Purchase a small black binder that includes notebook paper. This is to become your personal *Book of No's.* Each day you must write a brief summary of an event in which you said "no" to someone.

Write entries like this: "Today I said no to Ajax Mfg. Co. who wanted us to pay for 110,000 yards of goods at a higher price than we were quoted."

"Today I said no to a customer who asked for a two-year warranty when we customarily give only one year."

"Today I said no to my boss who asked me to fire the bookkeeper, because it is his responsibility to do that and not mine."

I began writing my own *Book of No's* four years ago when some personal pleasing actions on my part cost me dearly in the billfold. I had guaranteed the payment of loans and product shipments personally to a computer retailer in which I had a tiny investment in but where I served as chairman of the board. When the company failed, the lenders and vendors came after me to collect their money, and I not only had to pay them, but I had to pay lawyers to negotiate payment terms and to protect my assets.

It would have been simpler and smarter of me to tell the lenders and vendors, "If you want this business but need my personal guarantee, then you really don't want this business." I paid for my guilt toxicity, and I would rather be strapped buck naked to the town clock at midday than give my personal guarantee again.

HOW MICHAEL MILKEN TURNED JUNK INTO GOLD: THE LURE OF BIG-PROFIT DEALS

The junk bond craze of the 1980s owes its creation and development to Michael E. Milken, whose illegal activities are not endorsed herein, but whose deal-making abilities are. Milken was employed by a third-rate investment bank that, at the time Milken came aboard, had no significant corporate clients. Status on Wall Street is correlative with fee income, because the more prestigious the investment banker's client list, the more it can charge for its services. The top drawer investment banks derive enormous fees from raising capital and advising on mergers and acquisitions for their *Fortune* 500 clients. Milken's employer, Drexel Burnham Lambert, had marginal clients going into the 1980s, and its clout and profitability were destined to remain small for years to come because it was sacrosanct among the captains of American industry that their financial transactions be blessed with the imprimatur of Wall Street's finest—of which Drexel was not on the "approved" list.

Milken changed the financial markets and industrial management for years to come with a product, the junk bond, in a service industry.[*] The *junk bond* is a high interest rate—over 16 percent—usually unsecured bond, the interest and principal repayments of which are highly uncertain at best, and cannot be met at worst. Milken introduced junk bonds as the means for overpaying takeover targets in corporate raids. Typically, companies are taken over by entrepreneurs via leveraged buyouts that involve borrowing on the assets of the takeover target and repaying the borrowings out of the company's cash flow. The excess by which the price exceeds the amount that could be borrowed on the company's assets is typically 5 percent to 10 percent of the purchase price and funded by the entrepreneurial team. If the cash flow of the takeover is insufficient to service debt and pay back the risk equity and the entrepreneurs a reasonable return, a lower price is offered or the buyers walk away. Money rarely chased deals pre-Milken.

---

[*] Service spin-offs of product companies succeed more often than do product spin-offs of service companies.

"Though Drexel had not pioneered the LBO," writes Connie Bruck, "it was a match made in heaven. It was a philosophical fit: the LBO represented a shift of control from a bureaucratic organization into entrepreneurial hands. And it was an extension of what Milken had been doing since 1977, when he started to help his clients to leverage their balance sheets with high levels of debt, through the issuance of junk bonds."[*]

In dramatically over-paying for deals—by that I mean over twice the amount that could be borrowed on the target company's assets—Milken created a win-win-win situation for all of the participants in the takeover market:

1. *Secured Lenders:* The usual lenders in the leveraged buyout market were pleased with all of the takeover activity because their loans were fully secured and they were making lots more of them.

2. *Junk Bond Buyers:* Mutual funds, pension funds, insurance companies, and savings and loan institutions were thrilled to be loaning money at more than 16 percent interest. They were told that when an interest or principal payment came due, but could not be paid out of cash flow, Milken's firm would find a source of payment either by selling a peripheral division of the taken-over company or by selling additional securities to someone else.

3. *Managers of Taken-Over Companies:* Although some of them put up a semblance of a fight for public consumption, most managers had golden parachute deals that would make them multimillionaires posttakeover. Further, the takeovers were frequently at stock prices that they could not hope to generate in five years time, with even the most adroit management.

4. *Stockholders of Takeover Targets:* The owners of stock takeover targets were as happy as anyone could be who was being offered $1 for something that the most efficient auction market in economic history said was worth not a penny more than fifty cents. Stockholders of nontargets in the same industry benefited as well

---

[*] Bruck, Connie, *The Predator's Ball,* Simon & Schuster, New York, 1988, p. 99.

when their holdings rose in response to their *break-up value*: the projected aggregate price at which their company's parts would be broken off and sold.

5. *Investment Bankers:* The best deal of all fell in the lap of the investment bankers, of which Milken's firm, Drexel Burnham Lambert, became the most proficient, the most highly regarded, and the most profitable. Whereas investment banks traditionally earned one or two fees for arranging acquisitions for their corporate clients, Milken multiplied the number of fees to at least *six* per transaction and increased their size. The potpourri of his fees included the following:

   a. *Finder's fee* for introducing the target;

   b. *Valuation fee* charged to the buyer for stating that the price was "fair";

   c. *Financing fee* for raising the money to buy the company;

   d. *Equity fee,* or part ownership in the takeover target, for being its initiator;

   e. *Spin-off fees* (several, depending on the number of spin-offs earned by selling off divisions to raise cash); and

   f. *Refinancing fees* to refinance the junk bonds when it was clear to all that the debt could not be serviced.

Other investment banks jumped into the arena of enormously profitable activity created by Milken, like piranha at the carcass of a cow. Meanwhile, Milken's personal income exceeded $500 million per year on occasion. The competition to do Drexel-type deals in order to generate fees pushed the takeover game to such extreme ends that spin-offs and refinancings could not be done fast enough to stench the flow of blood. Commercial banks got sloppy and did not collateralize themselves properly. Companies were not managed by the raiders to maximize cash flow, and some of their trophies ended up in bankruptcy. "Junk bonds are by definition junk," said H. Ross Perot. "I didn't name them. The guys who created them named them. They are going to be worn like animals around the necks of the companies that sold them. They have nothing to do with anything except making fees."[*]

The premise of the junk-bond-backed LBO binge of the 1980s was simple: Let's overprice takeovers and see who buys the program. Nearly everyone whose name was called signed up for Milken's deals, notwithstanding that the entrepreneurs that the junk bonds were financing had unproven management ability. Names like Ronald Perelman, who acquired Revlon, Inc.; Nelson Peltz, who acquired Triangle Industries, Inc.; Carl Icahn, who acquired TWA, Inc.; T. Boone Pickens, who attempted to acquire Phillips Petroleum Corp.; and Bobby R. Inman, who acquired the Tracor Corp.

There have been some junk-bond-backed LBO bankruptcies, but for the most part the jury is on the side of the raiders. Putting aside the economic validity of the Milken-inspired age of takeover wretched excesses and ignoring the conviction of Milken for felonies that he committed during this period, the *deal* that he conceived, developed, implemented, and sold to some of the most astute lenders and investors in the country is awesome! One gapes in awe at the preposterousness of the Milken proposition, bought hook, line, and sinker by some of the most careful investors in the country.

Money managers entrusted with billions of dollars of savings and pension funds simply do not buy, in a rational world, junk bonds that yield 16 percent to 18 percent per year if the financial statements presented to them clearly indicate that there is inadequate cash flow to service the debt. Institutional investors are fiduciaries. Justice Louis Brandeis defined a fiduciary as someone to whom money is entrusted and who is supposed to exert greater care in its management than in the management of his or her own money. Why did these certified gatekeepers of the nation's savings take such incredible risks?

The *Godfather* Proposition

Milken (and the competitive investment bankers who tried to play catch-up to Drexel) made the institutional investors an offer, actually

---

[*] Mason, Todd, *Perot: An Unauthorized Biography*, Dow Jones, Inc., Homewood, Illinois, 1990, p. 10.

a series of offers, they could not refuse. First, they received a *commitment fee* upon subscribing to buy junk bonds. Thus, if the deal was lost to a competitive bidder, if the takeover broke down, or if the full amount of the financing could not be raised, the subscribing financial institution *received payment for reading the offering circular and documents.* The commitment fees ranged from 3/8 of 1 percent to 7/8 of 1 percent. Thus, a $10 million commitment resulted in a payment to the institution of approximately $50,000 for reading the deal and voting "yes."

Milken's junk bond offering circulars were shipped to institutional money managers in tightly bound manila envelopes with enough warnings on the outside about the responsibilities incurred by the recipient for reading the material in public, photocopying the enclosed materials, or disseminating them to third parties, to make one think that a time bomb and not a junk bond was inside. The packaging of a Drexel offering was unremitting in its warnings and therefore highly enticing. It screamed, "Open me, ye who seek undreamed of riches!"

The investor had to respond to a Drexel deal within 24 to 48 hours. Institutional investors were not used to being ordered about by investment bankers. But they took orders from Drexel. They either subscribed to the deal in two days, in order to see more junk bond deals in the future; or they could pass, and they would probably not see any more Drexel deals, unless perhaps they flew to Milken's Beverly Hills office and begged.

Milken changed the buyer-seller dynamics. Milken positioned junk bonds as solutions to the problems faced by institutional investors; that is, their need to earn sufficiently high yields to cover operating expenses and payouts to policy holders, pensioners, and passbook holders. Before Milken, if an institution could lock in average yields of 12 percent per annum it made ends meet. Junk bond yields of 16 percent to 18 percent were heaven sent because they permitted operating expenses (read: management salaries and bonuses) to rise without jeopardizing statutory payouts. An investment officer in a large institution frequently receives a bonus if his or her portfolio yields more than a predetermined target rate of return, such as 12 percent per year. A salaried investment officer earning $100,000 a year pre-Milken could bump his take-home pay by an additional

$100,000 by investing in junk bonds. That is a very strong induce-ment—the doubling of one's standard of living.

The final leg of the stool was Milken's tacit promise to junk bond buyers that, should the borrower be unable to pay interest or principal on the debentures when due, he and his team would either refinance the initial junk bond with a new one that offered superior features (read: greater promises), purchase their junk bond from them (that is, find a buyer if they wished to sell), or sell a peripheral division of the borrower to raise cash to meet the payment deadlines. Drexel had a highly skilled investment banking crew that was capable of "rolling over" the debt when it came due with debt restructurings or cashouts. Junk bond buyers and Drexel clients came to rely on Drexel's ability to perform miracles on interest and principal payment days; ability not shared by the competitive investment banks.

Drexel's promise to refinance junk bond principal when it came due was tantamount to a guarantee that the buyer would make and not lose money. Closings that involve guarantees are virtually the only way to sell marginal deals. We spoke about guarantees earlier. If you have to give one, you are a pleaser, and pleasers go out of business very quickly.

Drexel Ran Circles Around the Competition

There is no mistaking that Drexel ran rings around its competitors. Figure 10.1 lists the number and dollar amount of junk bond financings effected between 1984 and 1988 grouped by underwriter. Drexel's share of junk bond financings declined from 69 percent in 1984 to 41 percent in 1988, but it remained the dominant junk bond house.

THE DEMISE OF JUNK BONDS

To play catch-up ball, Drexel's competitors offered sweeteners to clients, offered yet higher prices to takeover targets, and embellished the junk bonds with equity kickers, higher interest rates and improved terms.

Figure 10.1
COMPETITION IN JUNK BOND UNDERWRITINGS
1984 to 1988 (a)

	$ Amount	Percentage
Drexel Burnham	$ 57.4 billion	45.9%
Morgan Stanley	13.5 billion	10.9
First Boston	10.9 billion	8.7
Merrill Lynch	10.6 billion	8.5
Other	50.8 billion	26.0
Total	$124.8 billion	100.0%

(a) Source: Investment Dealers Digest and Morris & Co., Incorporated. Reprinted here with permission.

The party that we came to know as the Great Takeover Bash of the late 1980s became a drunken brawl. All of the participants were making more money than they probably ever dreamed possible. Stockholders were selling out at double their investment. Managers were jumping out of taken-over companies and floating to the lush fairways of Scottsdale and Tarpon Springs on the gilded threads of golden parachutes. Institutional investors were showing more profits than at any time in their history, and their money managers' billfolds were crammed with the accolades of their financial acumen. The raiders built empires and sewed up net worths as large as their social security numbers. The investment bankers generated six to seven times the traditional fees of the business, and Milken alone made more money than the GNPs of half the countries in the United Nations.

Very little thought was given to the ability to repay over $260 billion in junk bonds. Some of the takeover targets hit craters in the road and defaulted. Some fraudulent inside trading by spotlight-needy characters in the arbitrage business—that is, investors who bet on takeovers—sent jitters through the institutional investor crowd. Congresspersons, who caused the savings and loan industry debacle by voting in 1982 to deregulate it without proper speed bumps, needed a scapegoat and blamed the Milken crowd and the junk bonds "that they forced on institutional investors." As quickly as the party began, it ended. Over 75,000 employees in the investment banking industry lost their jobs in 1989 and 1990. New York area real estate prices sank to record lows and pulled other markets down as well.

The Mechanics of Milken's Deal

The mechanics of Milken's innovation are worthy of serious review by deal-makers. Virtually single-handedly he created a $300 billion market in less than five years with the simplest of notions: Let's overpay for tired old companies and double everyone's expectations of their true personal worth and see who buys the program.

Milken never would have gotten off the ground if the institutional investors had not bought junk bonds. They were the *gatekeepers* in the dynamic, who possessed the marketplace leverage to charge Milken a toll to gain access to their billions of dollars. But Milken, and eventually his competitors, slicked the gatekeepers by paying them commitment fees, offering interest rates as high as twice the normal and customary tolls, and made outlandish promises, which were honored until Milken was dishonored, to protect the lenders from losing money on their loans. In one fell swoop, Milken unbolted the tollgates that protect the trillions of dollars of pensioners, passbook holders, and policyholders entrusted to fiduciaries, and tossed them on the side of the highway where the gatekeepers threw a celebratory feast for corporate raiders, and everyone toasted their acknowledged worth, which was at least twice what it was a few months prior.

The metamessage from the junk bond story leads us to the fourth axiom of closings:

> You can persuade people to do just about anything if you reward them with substantially more than their personal estimate of their own true worth.

CHAPTER 11

IT'S NOT WHO YOU KNOW, IT'S WHAT YOU KNOW ABOUT THEM

HOW TO MAKE THE MOST OF FINDERS

There are finders, brokers, dealers, and agents in nearly every market. The more difficult it is to locate buyers, the higher the finders fee. For instance, art dealers charge artists 50 percent for finding buyers. Real estate brokers charge 6 percent, and entertainment industry rights marketing agents charge 10 to 15 percent. The more difficult it is to locate buyers, then the higher the finders fee. There are hundreds of thousands of artists and sculptors attempting to place their work in the homes of collectors, who see the work for the most part in galleries. The gallery owners have gatekeeper leverage over the artists, worth a commission of 50 percent in most cases. Although the price is high, artists would be lost without dealers, at least when they are starting up, and require visibility and endorsement.

The key to choosing a finder to assist in closing your deal is to make certain that he or she will enhance, rather than detract from, the deal; that he or she can reduce or eliminate your "cost of search" by taking you right in to meet buyers; and that the finder's endorsement of you or your deal really means something.

This "ideal" finder that I am describing does not always exist at the appropriate time for you, but if he or she does, then you are almost assured of getting your deal money. Without him or her, the cost of search can be over $50,000. For instance, in a $20 million financing for an investment company start-up that I did in the early 1980s, I made visits to numerous pension fund and insurance company money managers to raise the deal money. It took seven presentations to obtain one $750,000 (average) commitment. To raise the entire $20 million, I had to make 210 presentations. Each presentation required a trip by car or airplane, but I generally made three presentations per day. Nonetheless, the cost of search came to about $75,000 or over $300 per presentation.

The buyers to whom I was presenting my deal were prequalified to be generically interested in my concept. However, they were new to me, and I was new to them. I did not use a finder to shoe-horn me in, and I was learning many of the closing strategies that are presented in this book.

At the beginning of my road show, my closing ratio was 1 in 10. At the end, it was 1 in 5. By the time that I completed the financing, I had one of the hottest Rolodexes of investors in investment companies in the country. But I no longer needed it because my deal had closed.

Finders, agents, brokers, and dealers continually add to and update their Rolodexes because they need to have a much better closing ratio than 1 in 5. If they can't do better than that, they begin to lose clients and soon fade from view.

DECIDE WHAT YOU HAVE ON WHO YOU KNOW

Accumulating the names of gatekeepers and buyers for the right Rolodex at the right time is very difficult to achieve. People change jobs, their responsibilities change within their organizations, and new buyers evolve into positions of power. Building and maintaining an up-to-the-minute Rolodex of the right buyers for the right deal is very difficult. The best finder may know from 5 percent to 25 percent of who they need to know when you need them to know it; but if that percentage is more than you know, then you need that finder.

This brings us to Axiom 5 in the deal-making business:

It's not so much what you've got. It's not even who you know.
What really counts is what you've got on who you know.

I have published several directories of sources of money and of
finders with access to sources of money, and I have attempted in
these directories to include substantive information about the buyers.
This information includes names of deals done, size of deals done,
industries of interest, other criteria; plus the names of companies in
which the buyer is involved—his or her board seats, previous employment, and college attended.

MULTICHANNEL DEAL CLOSING

I am a staunch advocate of multichannel marketing, and raising money
for a deal requires selling the deal in several markets at the same
time in order to maximize your chances of raising money. We can
borrow the style of the independent movie producer who works 10
money channels at the same time, first to finance the contracts with
the writer, star and director and then to finance the picture.

The same strategy applies to other kinds of deals. Catalog deals
involve testing multiple lists, statement stuffers, direct response advertising. The newsletter-seminar deal involves raising money via
subscriptions, ads in the newsletter and seminar selling. The new
business start-up involves networking in the community to tie in
people and institutions who stand to gain if your deal gets funded,
plus state loan programs, federal loan and grant programs, community
jobs-related funding sources, and venture capital.

Multichannel deal closing is the most efficient means of ac-
complishing the task. Just ask people with different Rolodexes to
find the money for you, and make a separate and distinct fee arrangement
with each one.

Each of the directories includes the usual name, address, telephone
number and FAX number, plus the names of the key decision-makers,
but also information to enable the deal person to get a *hook* and a
handle on the buyer. A name and address is a beginning but what
kind of deals does the buyer do? How many did the buyer do last

year? What were the sizes of these deals? What kinds of deals were they? What are the names and addresses of the companies that the buyer financed or provided deal money to? This is what I mean by "what you've got on who you know."

PREPARING YOUR BUSINESS PLAN

The choirbook that you and the finders will sing out of is the *business plan*. The goals and objectives of the deal must be clearly and concisely set forth in the business plan, along with the backgrounds of the management team and the relationships of the players who have endorsed the deal or who have contributed something to it or plan to do so once the deal is funded.

The business plan, and your oral presentations, must answer the following five questions:

1. How much can I make?
2. How much can I lose?
3. How do I get my money out?
4. Who says this deal is any good?
5. Who else is in it?

A deal person is selling a *concept* that he or she wants others to buy into. In this sense of the word, a concept salesperson is promoting an idea, a premise, a hypothesis. Thorough business plans are absolutely essential to closing your deal.

In asking the five questions, the buyer is attempting to accept or reject the business plan quickly to maximize his or her time. It is in his or her interest, as much as that of the entrepreneur, to avoid 30 days of investigation that results in a turndown. Thus the investor is inclined to turn down a deal quickly if the answers to these five questions are not what he or she was looking for.

For example, if the operating statement projections are too flat, the deal could be turned down because the rate of return is inadequate. Or if the projection ramp is too steep, the turndown may be the result of unrealistic projections. The answer to the question "How much can I lose?" has to do with the use of proceeds of the financing. The entrepreneur may need product development money at a time when the investor has an excess of development stage risk in his or her portfolio. To the third question, "How do I get my money out?" the investor wonders if this company can be taken public, or sold to a larger company—the conventional means of capitalizing on an investment—or if it will be a cash cow. When the investor asks the next question about management track record he or she would like the answer to be that the entrepreneurs were involved in the founding of Hewlett-Packard or Weight Watchers International and that they have blessed this investor with the opportunity to finance their second company. This does not happen on a daily basis, and in fact investors are faced with lesser-of-evil choices most of the time because most entrepreneurs have trackrecords ranging from none to poor. What the investor likes to see, however, is that the entrepreneur exhibits the judgment to hire skilled managers, primarily in the areas of marketing, manufacturing, finance, and engineering. The purpose of the fifth question is for the investor to find others who have endorsed the company by agreeing to provide products, credit, contracts, or purchases.

If all of this sounds wooden and mechanical, then pray tell how one Fred Smith, aged 29, raised $96 million from Prudential Insurance, General Dynamics, and 26 venture capital funds to launch Federal Express Corporation in the pit of the 1973 recession on the basis of a term paper he had written in college and without any substantive previous business experience. Some small companies have trouble paying for postage, while others have to send back offers to invest because they are oversubscribed. Apple Computer Corporation raised more venture capital in 1978–1980 than the rest of the personal computer industry in total, although it is not reputed to manufacture the best hardware or offer the most useful software. Its founders were two unseasoned engineers under age 26, but the manager they hired to run Apple, Michael Markulla, was considered one of the marketing stars at Intel Corporation, and he attracted venture capital from Arthur Rock and others. Peter Farley, the molecular biologist who founded Cetus Corporation, raised over $36 million from industrial corporations and venture capitalists in the mid-1970s and then $125 million from the public in early 1981, without a product or more than a few million dollars in contracts. Dr. Leonard Schoen, the founder of Arcoa Corporation, operator of the U-Haul System of one-way truck and trailer rentals, has raised all of Arcoa's capital privately through tax-shelter oriented limited partnerships that own the trucks and trailers and lease them to the company. The seed capital for *Psychology Today* came very rapidly from recipients of a direct mail test who subscribed to the magazine at an overwhelming rate, thus providing the cheapest of all forms of capital: customers' money. Yet in the shadow of these success stories lies the wreckage of thousands of economically viable, socially useful businesses that have been unable to attract financing.

Getting the Meeting

Many entrepreneurs use finders to submit their business plans and arrange meetings. Sponsorship is the best means of getting the meeting. Naturally there is a fee, but it is usually worthwhile to pay 5 percent if the chance of raising capital depends on it. If one is without the services of a financial intermediary, it is advisable to deliver the business plan in person and attempt to sell the credit at the first meeting while the lender skims the material. In order to get the appointment the entrepreneur should ask the lender or investor if "I may come by and drop off the material." At that point, the prospect will probably reply with, "Why don't you just mail it and I'll give you a call after I have read it." Persistence and tenacity are appreciated by lenders and investors, and the entrepreneur should rebut with, "I have to be near your office tomorrow anyway, and it wouldn't be out of my way to drop it off." This proposal might fit neatly into the potential backer's schedule, but assuming it does not, the entrepreneur can choose one of several other options:

1. "If the afternoon is not good for you, I can change my other appointment and see you in the morning."

2. "If tomorrow is not acceptable, I need to be back your way in one or two days." (Leaving options open.)

3. "I have lunch open on my schedule if that would be a convenient time."
4. "If your schedule is tight right now, why don't we get together for breakfast?"
5. "Perhaps you could squeeze me in after work one day this week."

I firmly believe that lenders and investors are more interested in tenacious deal persons than in relaxed or casual ones. Self-confidence reflects positively on the concept you are promoting. Intimidation mixed with charm is an excellent initial impression to make on an investor or lender. For example, if the person absolutely will not see you, you might laughingly say something like, "Gee, you guys must have a lot of good deals in there now."

In attempting to arrange the meeting, the entrepreneur must be careful to balance persistence with politeness so as not to appear "pushy." You want to create an image of being busy and important—running off to meetings with other lenders, customers, suppliers, lawyers, and advertising agents. If nothing seems to be working, but the lender or investor still has not hung up the telephone, you might take a few minutes to explain the key ingredients, entrepreneurial team, market size, and product niche. If this is indeed interesting, then the listener will try to find time for a meeting.

12

TURNING
NO INTO *YES:*
DON'T LET THEM
WEAR YOU DOWN

THE CLOSING BEGINS WITH *NO*

All deal-makers are turned down frequently, abruptly, and without explanation. It took the producers of Academy Award winner *Chariots of Fire* five years to find someone with a checkbook to say yes. Oliver Stone required eight years of repetitive turndowns to find the financing for *Platoon,* which won an Academy Award for best movie. Raymond Kroc, founder of McDonald's Corp., met with continual failure for the first 50 years of his life before driving out to San Bernardino, California, one day in the 1950s to find out why a certain drive-in restaurant owned by the McDonald brothers was ordering so many milkshake machines, a product he was then selling.

Turndowns and bad times make deal men and women work smarter. No one ever held onto a fortune if it came too easily. Wealth is made in hard times. As Nietzche wrote, "It takes a chaos to make a shooting star."

The founders of Sony Corp., Masaru Ibuka and Akio Morita, began their company by developing a rice cooker. They produced 100 of them, all of which burned the rice. Everyone turned them down. To survive, Morita sold his dilapidated Datsun truck for $500 and spent the money to develop Ibuka's idea for a consumer tape recorder.

He had seen a military tape recorder one day in Occupation Headquarters, and the idea began to take shape in 1948. But Ibuka had no patents, no recorder, and no tape. Japan had no plastic, and an import license was not permitted. Thus, Ibuka and Morita had to create the technology of magnetizing tape and of capturing sound on it. They did just that, and when they had created this unique innovation, nobody wanted it; because, as Ibuka and Morita were to have etched in their brains via their thin billfolds, nobody would need this innovation until sold on the idea of the need.

Out of sheer desperation, Morita stepped into the proverbial phone booth, changed clothes, and blasted out of the phone booth as one of the greatest salespeople the electronics industry has ever seen. He called on schools, government agencies, individuals in their homes, and shopkeepers, always listening to the customer while accepting the turndown. Finally, he found a secret: A new product must be a solution to a problem in order to generate sales. The need that Morita found was education, and Sony Corporation's tape recorder began to penetrate Japanese schools in the early 1950s. The company quickly penetrated other markets; then Ibuka became concerned that the technological brains he had assembled would grow bored without new challenges. He flew to America to explore transistor technology in 1953, and for $25,000, Ibuka purchased a license from Bell Laboratories to use transistors. On the ride home, Ibuka became fixated with another idea: "Radios small enough so each individual will be able to carry them around for his own use, with power that will enable civilization to reach even those areas with no electric power."*

MITI (The Ministry of International Trade and Industry) prevented Ibuka from patenting the idea, saying that if transistorized radios were such a good idea why had Hitachi and Toshiba failed to build them. Ibuka kept his engineers busy developing radios, while he put his documentation together to persuade MITI to change its mind. The arguments prevailed a year later, and Ibuka and his chief engineer

* Nick Lyons, *The Sony Vision,* Crown, New York, 1976, p. 41.

then left for the United States to learn all they could about photographic etching and advanced crystallography. After three months, Ibuka returned, but his chief engineer remained. Each day he telephoned Ibuka about the things he had learned at conferences and in laboratories. In 1954, Texas Instruments, Inc. (TI) announced the first transistorized radio. Although it initially jarred Ibuka, he used the defeat as fuel to galvanize his team and himself into a mindset that created heroic achievements. Thereafter, all major breakthroughs in consumer electronics for nearly 30 years were to come from Sony, as it rocketed past Hitachi, Toshiba, Matsushita (Panasonic), TI, RCA Corporation, Westinghouse Electric Corporation, and General Electric Company. Notwithstanding Sony Corporation's higher-priced transistor radio—$40 per unit versus TI's $12.95—Sony Corporation was delivering *consumer satisfaction*. It advertised "the radio that works." To stay ahead, Ibuka badgered his engineers and production chiefs to make the radio smaller and smaller. He wanted a pocket radio. His experts said it was impossible, but Ibuka was relentless in his desire.

From its successes in transistor radios, Sony Corporation was able to fund the development and manufacture of the Trinitron one-lens color TV (1968) and the Betamax VCR in 1975. Thereafter have come the Tummy TV, the Walkman, a musical calculator, a personal computer, the Mavica digital disc still camera, the Digital Audio Disc system, the BVP 330 professional video camera, and a fully-equipped van to permit film editing in under 10 days.

Finding the Rhythm of the Deal

"That guy could turn around a turndown better than any other deal man who ever walked in here," I have heard lending officers say in describing a particularly effective loan closer.

Turning "no" into "yes" is the particular skill of successful dealmakers and they do it by controlling the *cadence* of the deal.

Every deal has a form and a rhythm. The form defines the deal—an entrepreneurial start-up, a movie produced independently, a leveraged buyout, or refinancing of a bank loan. The rhythm of the deal is the cadence by which it flows from initial conception to final closing. Slow responses from helpers, joint-venturers, and lenders or buyers usually means that the deal is not going very well. You can sense in your telephone call-backs that if the lender or investor is particularly difficult to contact or to get calls back from, your deal is probably not getting a serious look. Something is amiss, and you can *hear* it in the nonreplies or slow and infrequent call-backs. If your deal is bogged down in the quagmire of poor responses, then something is wrong with it. Visit one of the buyers and level with him or her. Ask him or her to tell you what's missing in your deal. It could lead to a turnaround when you have an opportunity to run it back through after making some adjustments.

Befriend the Secretary

How do you get a meeting if nobody returns your telephone calls? The first thing you must do is get around the buyer's secretary. There are one hundred and one ways to do this, from outright bribery to pretending to be someone else on the telephone, but I do not condone the fake-caller tactic because it reflects poorly on the deal-maker as one who is clever but not sound.

I would fax or telephone the buyer (before the secretary arrives or after she leaves) and ask for help. This is the "mouse asking the lion how to survive in the jungle" strategy. When applied to the potential buyer, it goes something like this:

"Sorry to interrupt you, Mr. Buyer, but I must have sent you the worst deal you've ever seen because I have been calling you for two weeks and I haven't had a response."

"Who is this?" the buyer asks.

"This is David Silver, and I submitted the deal where city streets would be replaced by steel plates that sit on top of magnets, and people walking and cars driving on them would automatically generate enough energy to power the cities, and our reliance on foreign oil or all fossil fuels would diminish."

"You say you sent this deal in?" the buyer asks, and you can hear the ruffling of papers in the background.

"About two weeks ago. It's in a green cover," you say.

"Here it is. I remember. It really doesn't fit what we are trying to do here, so..."

"Excuse me for cutting in, but I don't think the deal as described is meeting anyone's criteria. There's something wrong with it, or in the way I have described it," you interject.

"Could be," he says, indicating that he really didn't get past the first page or else he would have had specific reasons for the turndown.

"If I could buy you breakfast someday, and you tell me what day works for you, I would like your advice on how to put my deal together, or kill it once and for all. Would you do that for me?" you ask.

"Well, I'm very busy at this time..."

"But everybody's got to eat. What about lunch? I'll bring in some sandwiches. And you can take calls, be interrupted, and do your normal routine, just as long as I could pick your brain for 30 minutes."

"Well..."

"How about it? Turkey on rye?"

THE *IF-THEN-WHAT* QUESTIONS

To turn a turndown around, it is important to know the exact reasons for the turndown and then overturn each obstacle. The following story tells how one entrepreneur persistently worked a "no" into a "yes."

"I think I have written a good business plan," the entrepreneur said to me. "The product sells fairly well without much marketing money—we will do $800,000 in our third year of operations—I have built a strong team, young but bright and eager. Yet every venture capitalist we go to turns us down. How can I raise venture capital?"

This is the answer I gave him: "You have to turn the turndowns around. There is an expression in lending: 'He wouldn't accept a turndown.' Some deals do not read very well and fail to impress investors and lenders, but the entrepreneur will not permit himself to be turned down. He keeps coming back with the 'if-then-what' questions until he gets the money.

"Avoiding the turndown requires finding out from the least hostile and most helpful investor the precise reasons for his turndown. The entrepreneur responds with, 'Okay, if I jump through the hoop, what will you do?' The venture capitalist generally says, 'Come back and we'll review it.'

"The entrepreneur returns and says, 'I did the thing you asked me to do, now what can I do to get you to invest?' This give and take goes on and on for as many visits as necessary until the venture capitalist visits the entrepreneur's facility. At this point, he is on the entrepreneur's turf and off his own, thus less defensive and more open to the idea of investing. He can be closed, or at least give a conditional commitment."

A typical turndown turnaround might go as follows:

Entrepreneur: Why?

Venture Capitalist: You haven't convinced me that you can sell the product, that there's a market for it. You have too much debt in the company senior to my position. You can have a deficit net worth. And I think I can make more money with other investments.

Entrepreneur: If I were to correct the things you object to to your satisfaction, would you then come out to visit the plant and meet the management team?

Venture Capitalist: Yes, but you're facing an uphill battle. I have many attractive opportunities. This is a busy time for me. And your deal is not what I'm looking for.

Entrepreneur: May I at least try to convince you? Will you take my calls as long as they are to inform you that I have corrected your objections?

Venture Capitalist: I will take your calls if that's what they're about.

Time passes, during which the entrepreneur calls his sales force and puts on a full court press to generate orders. Since the company cannot produce the orders thus generated, the entrepreneur must visit the key suppliers and ask them for more credit. If they refuse, or if some of them refuse, the entrepreneur will have to go to his board or private investors and tell them that a venture capitalist has indicated a preliminary interest in investing—this is a long leap, but entrepreneurs, after all, are said to be people who record a receivable before they make a sales call—subject to certain conditions being met. The board or local investors agree to a *bridge financing*, a short-term loan to accomplish a goal and to be repaid when the goal is achieved. Sometimes bridge financing becomes *permanent capital*, which demonstrates far greater faith in the company.

With $100,000 in bridge financing, the entrepreneur can comfortably reach out for more orders, even run some advertising, and move sales up to a higher plateau. After a few months of higher sales, one or two suppliers may agree to extend more credit, which has the effect of allowing sales to grow to a still higher level. It is time to call the venture capitalist.

Entrepreneur: We have taken sales from $200,000 per month when I was in your office to $450,000 per month. I can maintain this level, but I cannot go higher.

Venture Capitalist: How did you increase sales?

Entrepreneur: My board plus two outside investors bought $100,000 of subordinated notes which the company can call at 150 percent of face value after one year. They have the right to put at the same price. Or they can convert the $100,000 into 5 percent of the company's stock. We then got two suppliers to raise their credit limits from $100,000 to $150,000. Several other suppliers have agreed to go out to 75 days from 60 days, which allows us to work with their money. We put new people into our receivables department who have brought average receivables days down from 52 to 36, so we're turning our cash faster. I cannot improve on receivables or supplier terms more than this. I can get sales up another 75 percent when we raise prices next month, but without long-term capital, we're stopped at this point.

Venture Capitalist: Sounds like you're on the right track. Where did the sales growth come from?

Entrepreneur: We opened several new markets with reps: the Northeast, Northern Middle West, and Pacific Northwest. We hired regional sales managers for these territories and trained the reps. The sales managers were given low bases and 10 percent overrides on the first $500,000 of new sales and 5 percent thereafter. The reps have standard commissions plus premiums for meeting goals, such as a trip to Hawaii. In our traditional markets, we have offered regular customers sharper discounts for volume orders and set up a series of premiums for the salespeople and reps there as well, with the top prizes of two Super Bowl tickets and a week in Mexico City. We began running national ads in five monthly trade magazines, and we took a larger booth at one of the regional trade shows.

Venture Capitalist: It seems to be working. Send me a list of customers with telephone numbers. I want to find out why they're buying.

Entrepreneur: Okay, and I'll send along about 20 product endorsements that we've gotten recently, as well as a comparison study done by one of the trade magazines that shows how we compare with the competition.

Venture Capitalist: How are you doing with the debt problem and the deficit net worth?

Let us assume that the company had cumulative losses of $1,000,000 and a $1,200,000 FmHA guaranteed term loan secured by plant and equipment as well as a line of credit from a commercial finance company secured by accounts receivable and inventory. Its balance sheet looks something like Figure 12.1.

The balance sheet portrays a company at the bottom but near the vertical portion of its S-curve, starved for expansion capital. To convince the venture capitalist to climb aboard, the entrepreneur has to eliminate the deficit and retire some senior debt. We assume that the company has been delinquent in its interest and principal payments to the FmHA. That is the logical place to discuss a refinancing.

The entrepreneur visits the FmHA and the bank and explains that the likelihood of the company becoming current on interest and principal is slim unless it can take in venture capital. In fact, a

Figure 12.1
BALANCE SHEET BEFORE WORKOUT FINANCING

ASSETS		LIABILITIES AND NET WORTH	
Cash	$ 27,500	Accounts Payable, Accruals	$ 238,000
Accounts Receivable	175,000	Notes Payable	240,000
Inventories	342,000	Current Portion Long-Term Debt	200,000
Prepaid Deposits	40,500		
Total Current Assets	585,000	Total Current Liabilities	678,000
Net Plant, Equipment	350,500	20-Year Term Loan Guaranteed by FmHA	1,000,000
Other Assets	7,000	Investors Subordinated Debt	100,000
		Total Liabilities	1,778,000
		Capital Stock	175,000
		Accumulated Deficit	(1,010,500)
		Stockholders' Equity	(835,500)
TOTAL ASSETS	$942,500	TOTAL LIABILITIES & STOCKHOLDERS EQUITY	$ 942,500

venture capitalist made that clear to the company after 30 others had turned down the deal out of hand.

The entrepreneur proposes that the FmHA and bank release the collateral to enable the company to do a sale and leaseback to an affiliated company. The company will then give the FmHA $600,000, or 50 percent, of its loan in cash and the remainder on a 15-year 2 percent sales royalty. The balance sheet effect, if the plant and equipment are sold for $900,000, is a $600,000 forgiveness of debt and a $300,000 injection of capital by the stockholders, seen in Figure 12.2.

Figure 12.2
BALANCE SHEET AFTER WORKOUT FINANCING

ASSETS		LIABILITIES AND NET WORTH	
Cash	$327,500	Accounts Payable, Accruals	$ 238,000
Accounts Receivable	175,000	Notes Payable	240,000
Inventories	342,000		
Prepaid Deposits	40,500		
Total Current Assets	885,000	Total Current Liabilities	478,000
Other Assets	7,000	Investors Subordinated Debts	
			100,000
		Total Liabilities	578,000
		Capital Stock	475,000
		Accumulated Deficit	(410,500)
		Stockholders' Equity	315,000
TOTAL ASSETS	$892,000	TOTAL LIABILITIES & STOCKHOLDERS EQUITY	$892,000

The entrepreneur must be extremely persuasive to the government and the lead bank. They are not in the business of taking write-offs gratuitously. However, they respect the numbers, and in this case the numbers show that the company cannot pay off their loan without venture capital, which will not come into the company unless they agree to get off the balance sheet in a manner that adds to net worth. The entrepreneur returns to the venture capitalist and shows what he has done.

Venture Capitalist: I'll invest $600,000 if the bridge money converts.

Entrepreneur: We've gotten this far, I'm sure they'll agree to do it.

PART THREE

SPECIAL DEALS

This last section concerns itself with difficult deals, and difficult deals require tenacity. A word or two about being tough when times are hard. There are quite a few quotes that businesspeople keep on their desks to remind them that when the going gets tough, the tough get going; or the impossible just takes a little longer; or eagles don't flock, you have to catch them one at a time.

These aphorisms may be fine to keep you charged up during the day when your dobber is down. Heaven knows, we all need our heroic phrases to help us through tough times. But what the deal-maker needs to remember is not to keep these one-liners in his memory bank, but to let the buyer know a few zingers once in awhile. Let the buyer know of your tenacity in word and deed.

One of my favorites is the deal person's response to the buyer who invited him to fly back to Chicago to present his story to the buyer's committee. "If I fly, you buy," said the deal-maker.

"What is that supposed to mean?" asked the buyer.

"Just that," said the seller. "If I spend $1,200 to visit you again, I expect to close the deal. Are you willing to help me make that happen, because I don't like to waste money?"

The buyer can respond to that with his inability to commit, and the need for a second meeting, and "No guarantees. You come on your nickel and take a chance." But in reality, he or she cannot help but appreciate the deal person's need to know he or she is making an expensive trip for the purpose of closing the deal.

Tenacity is a state of mind: One either cares deeply that he or she is going to close the deal, or not. A buyer can sense it. He or she can smell it. He or she can feel it when the seller enters the room. "This guy won't take a turndown," I have said to myself many times upon meeting a deal man for the first time. "He works me, and works me, and I know he is going to arm-twist, cajole, persuade, and compromise with everyone he does business with."

Tenacious entrepreneurs *need* the deal to happen. Consequently, they make the deal happen. They don't let up. They work everyone constantly, on the telephone, in person, and by mail and courier. Buyers like that. It makes them feel that no amount of adversity will stand in the way of this person because he or she is too tenacious to let things get in his or her way for too long.

13

BONEYARD REAL ESTATE DEALS

For those of you with the deal-maker's heart, the courage of a lion, but billfolds as thin as a razor blade, there is the *boneyard deal*. This means buying a property or a company that is in so much trouble and so mired in litigation and risk that nobody in his or her right mind would touch it. But you need a deal, and if you can cut through the crises, cash will flow.

Reynold M. Sachs, formerly an economics professor at Columbia University, was called in to Digital Switch Corp. in the late 1970s to untangle the webs and set the company on a proper course. He retired a few years later in his early forties when Digital's stock reached $60 on NASDAQ.

Sam Zell, sometimes referred to as the "gravedancer" because of his love for buying troubled companies, purchased the bankrupt railcar leasing company Itel Corp. in 1983 and has used it as an acquisition vehicle for other deals.

Some of the greatest deals have been struck in the boneyards between courageous deal-makers and worried stockholders or managers who feel "tar-babied" to a company that is mired in illiquidity and litigation. Along comes B'rer Rabbit and they will pay him to take the deal off their hands.

In troubled times, you can walk through the corporate boneyard and buy ruined or merely frightened companies very inexpensively.

The excitement in boneyard buying is being cheap, tight, penny-pinching, niggardly—throwing dimes on the table as if they were manhole covers. When asked by the seller's lawyer to improve the offer, say no. In tough times part of the reason companies are in trouble is that their managers said yes when they should have said no.

In boneyard buying, you don't know how much worse the economy might become. You are piling on mountains of debt to make an acquisition that in itself is speculative and uncertain, but the acquisition you are making is supposed to generate life-saving cash. Therefore, you must be so tight with your commitments, money, and guarantees that you squeak when you walk. If it is not your style to be tough and tight, then you probably won't be good at boneyard buying.

FINDING UNDERVALUED RETAIL SITES

There is a story, probably at least half-legend, that a German brewer who emigrated to America in the middle of the nineteenth century figured out where to set up his saloons by selecting corner locations near the curbs most worn down by foot traffic. It was, apparently, a good idea (the forerunner of traffic counts), and his name, Joseph Schlitz, is on a lot of beer.

Identifying undervalued real estate investments requires the kind of time, energy, and creativity that Joseph Schlitz spent. Some investors do traffic counts with quick eyes and stop watches, painstakingly counting the number of people who pass by a particular location in an hour or a day, even analyzing the hours traffic is heaviest. Such analysis can spell the difference between a successful business and a dismal failure.

One location, for example, may be passed by numerous automobiles in the morning. Across the street, a second location may be passed by people on their way home. A traffic light may even stop the morning and evening rush hour traffic in front of both locations. The first location might be a gold mine for a Dunkin' Donuts franchisee, while the second would probably do better as a Kentucky Fried Chicken outlet. Reverse the two stores and they'd both probably fail for lack of customers.

Ask any real estate salesperson about the three most important factors in his or her business and you'll get the same answer every time: location, location, location. This is your first key to finding properties for yourself. Just look around your own community. Are the retail businesses located to conveniently serve the greatest number of customers? Is the office supply store located near offices? Are the florists mingled in with other shops so passersby can be drawn in by the beautiful window displays? Which retailers do best in malls, which on busy side streets, which ones downtown, which in the suburbs?

How will such analysis help you? It will give you the information you need to spot "obvious" opportunities. For example, federal post offices in most cities are so poorly situated that entrepreneurs have been doing very well opening mail and package-handling centers in suburban shopping centers. While charging a premium for postage and handling, they save the person who needs daily postal service or a PO box the trouble and cost of driving downtown to the post office. Retail service companies are extremely location-sensitive.

Who shops at a particular store is often as important as how many people shop there. Retail businesses that men visit more than women—computer, home improvement, hardware, and athletic equipment stores, for instance, are usually located *near* enclosed malls, but rarely *within* them. Why? Because men don't like to shop in enclosed malls as much as women do. Which is why shops more heavily frequented by women—apparel, shoe, fabric, craft, and toy stores—*are* in malls.

How they shop is also a factor. People on foot like to shop on the sunny side of streets to avoid the cooler, shady sides. If a retail establishment caters to automobile traffic, it must offer parking.

In your search for undervalued real estate, look for retail establishments that are poorly situated and going out of business because they are located inconveniently, lack parking, are on the wrong side of the street, and so forth. The current owner of such a property may be having trouble finding tenants that stick around and may be ready to throw up his or her hands and sell the location to you. Assuming that you don't have very much money, you may be able to negotiate a small-scale leveraged buyout—borrowing the money to buy the property from a bank, secured lender, or even the seller, and then repaying it from the cash flow of the tenant(s) that you locate. (If you haven't located a tenant before you have signed the Purchase and Sales Agreement and loan papers, you may even be able to get a grace period of 90 to 100 days in which you do not have to make payments on the loan.)

BUYING DISTRESSED PROPERTIES

If you like and have the ability to renovate houses, consider buying a house on which the bank is about to foreclose. You can often buy such properties at a substantial discount from the principal amount of the loan—say, 20 cents on the dollar—fix them up yourself and resell them, paying off the loan and keeping the difference as your profit. Many real estate fortunes have been made by entrepreneurs who started just this way. Since this is a road to wealth, young people can consider traveling *right now*—over summer vacation or even after school—let's discuss it in more detail.

When homeowners get into financial difficulty and cannot meet their mortgage payments for five or six months in a row, the bank that holds the mortgage, after several warnings, will normally foreclose on the loan. After all, a mortgage loan is a secured loan and the real estate—the home and land around it—is the collateral.

Banks normally contact a real estate broker to sell the foreclosed real estate for them in an attempt to recoup the principle amount of their loan. (By the way, real estate taxes are frequently owing on the property as well, and taxes represent a priority lien on the property, which means they must be paid first. Real estate taxes are assessed by the county to pay for schools, roads, street lights, the sheriff's department, and so forth. You can visit the county clerk's office and get a list of addresses of properties on which taxes are owed, then visit them to see which ones you may wish to purchase when they are sold at the local courthouse.)

If there are several properties in a run-down section of town near the main street, you may want to purchase the bank's mortgage loan and agree to pay the county its taxes, both on a work-out or stretch-out basis. This means that you will make regular payments to the bank and to the county, but in smaller monthly payments than the original loan called for. In the case of taxes, which are normally due all at once, you may be able to pay them over 6 to 12 months. You can then use the cash you have now to renovate the property, perhaps creating commercial space—art galleries, restaurants, and so forth—on the first floor and residences on the upper floors, rent the property to tenants (whose credit references you carefully check, of course, with TRW or Dun & Bradstreet), and create perceived value for the property.

As a result of your hard work, other attractive shops, perhaps antique stores, an ice cream parlor, and/or a clothing store, will move into the area. Within several years you can sell the property for a price two or three times more than the principle amount of the mortgage.

The great thing about buying and renovating distressed property is that *you do not have to use much capital to begin with.* You substitute labor for capital, and with a paint stripper, wallpaper steamer, paint brush, paint, hammer, nails and a saw, you can turn a blighted neighborhood into a beautiful, valuable section of town. The use of your personal labor to create value is called sweat equity. Not only will you benefit financially, but you will have given a gift to your community.

HOW TO START DEALS IN REAL ESTATE

Because it is *fungible,* readily transferable to another owner and, therefore, near-liquid, real estate is perhaps the most acceptable collateral to banks, insurance companies, savings and loan institutions, and other lenders. Since it is an appreciating asset, rather than a depreciating one, a lender will usually loan as much as 80 percent of the appraised value of real estate. Real estate appraisers visit the property and examine it, then visit comparable properties in the neighborhood to ascertain what prices they have sold for recently. After that, they prepare their *appraisal* for the person or bank who requested it, and the financing moves forward from that point. The lender indicates how much money it will advance to the buyer and secures this advance with a *first mortgage* loan, a security interest in the property that is recorded in the county clerk's office.

Let's see how these numbers work out. Assume the appraised value of your new property is $100,000 and the lender tells you that it will loan you 80 percent or $80,000, against the property. That means you still need $20,000 to buy the property, plus whatever is necessary to renovate it; let's presume that's another $75,000 for a total of $95,000 in all.

After renovating the property with sweat equity or hired labor and getting one or more tenants to occupy the property, it is fairly certain that the property will increase in value. The lender knows that and it will, in most circumstances, provide a construction loan to enable the property to be renovated by a skilled contractor. So you've got your $75,000. When the renovation is completed, the appraiser is called back to reappraise the property. Most likely, it is worth twice its original value and the lender will roll the construction loan, which is a short-term loan, into the first mortgage loan. This will make the first mortgage loan worth $155,000 ($80,000 plus $75,000).

If the new appraised value is $200,000, your equity in the property has increased from the $20,000 (the only money you had to put up for this whole deal) to $45,000 ($200,000 minus $155,000). Your capital gain is $25,000—more than 100 percent in just a few months. Based on the other kinds of investments we have been discussing, very few are both fungible (almost liquid) and capable of doubling your investment in a couple of months.

But you're a cash-poor student. And you're still short $20,000. Where is that down payment supposed to come from? That is an excellent question. There are three sources for the $20,000:

1. You can find partners who have the $20,000 or part of it to coinvest in the property with you.

2. The seller of the property may provide seller financing; that is, he or she will hold onto a security interest that is subordinated to the bank's first mortgage and permit you to repay him or her over time, say five years, out of the cash flow (rental payments) from the property. This is known as a second mortgage. Or—

3. There are second mortgage lenders who are willing to provide most of the $20,000 in consideration for a high interest rate—perhaps 2 percent higher than the interest rate paid to the bank for the first mortgage—over a short period of time (three to five years).

In other words, you might be able to buy the $100,000 property for only $2,000 of your own capital. The $18,000 you borrow for your down payment (from one of the three sources mentioned) reduces your capital gain to $27,000 ($45,000 minus $18,000), but that means you have multiplied the money you actually invested yourself—only $2,000, remember—13.5 times in just a few months. That is a remarkable rate of return!

Before you rush out and sell your baseball cards, Presleyana and the savings bonds that Uncle Herman gave you for your sixth birthday and buy the first rundown building you can find for $2,000, let's review the subject of leverage. Remember what we said about managers of publicly-held companies who borrow more debt than they are able to service. They were taking high levels of risk, perhaps more risk than necessary. The same applies to leveraging $98,000 on top of your $2,000 investment. If the value of the property suddenly declines or if your tenants leave and you cannot replace them, then it is quite possible that you will be unable to make the payments on your first and second mortgage loans. Then the lenders will foreclose on your property and you will lose your $2,000 investment.

Leverage, in other words, cuts two ways: It works well when values are rising, but it can cut a big hole in your billfold when values are falling. (Which is why real estate investors love inflation, a time when prices of goods and services—and real estate is good—increase without an increase in their inherent value.)

My Boneyard Deal

One of the nation's largest corporations with sales of $15 billion decided to divest itself of all peripheral divisions to raise cash for its core business, paper products. I heard about a manufacturing division in the Southwest that the corporation was selling. The company manufactured wallboard. The corporation had invested over $2 million in equipment and product and another $500,000 in obtaining product approvals from the two agencies that test all products that go into buildings.

On top of that, the corporation had operated the wallboard division for two and one-half years, but it had never earned a profit. In fact, it lost $600,000 in the aggregate on average sales of $3 million per annum.

I called the divestiture officer at the corporation and asked to see the Selling Memorandum. After signing a Confidentiality Agreement, two inches of computer-generated cash flow statements and equipment lists were sent to me along with a three-page memorandum that summarized the business. I scheduled an appointment at the plant with a junior officer in the divestiture department, and following a walk-through, we sat down in the rather sparse offices of the plant manager to discuss price.

Papers and documents were being boxed for shipment to a warehouse, so I knew that if the divestiture officer couldn't sell the business, he was going to shut it down and auction off the equipment. Thus, my competition was not another bidder, but rather liquidation value. I knew my first call after leaving the plant had to be to an equipment appraiser to purchase a liquidation value appraisal; that is, the appraiser's estimate of what the equipment would bring at auction. From that I would deduct my estimate of what it would cost the corporation to cancel its plant lease, then deduct a dollar estimate for the cost of moving the equipment to an auctioneer's warehouse and I would know my bid, and I knew it would be the winning bid; if not immediately, then eventually.

The divestiture officer said he was looking for a price of $1,350,000. I asked what he based the "ask" on. He said, "The book value of the equipment on the plant floor is $960,000, and the difference is the cost of obtaining your own approval codes."

He went on about the $2,500,000 that the corporation invested in developing a unique product line and in developing innovative manufacturing equipment. He showed me the customer list. I asked for permission to contact the customers directly, and he granted it.

I asked if he would permit the acquiring company to sell product under the corporation's approval codes until we obtained ours. He said he would attempt to get that approval for me. I said it would be a deal breaker if I didn't have it. He understood.

I said I would get back to him in a week with an offer. He countered that he was instructed to sell the plant or close it if he could not find a buyer within two weeks. I said I understood. He then said that there were other buyers who were in the business who were moving quickly toward making a bid. I said, "There usually are," but that I would respond promptly "as soon as I had an equipment appraisal."

Within a week I received a "desktop" appraisal of $396,000 from a well-known appraiser. He said, "I'll type it up and ship it up to you; but that's the number: $396,000."

I contacted the landlord to attempt to ascertain if he was going to hang tough on the two and one-half years remaining on the lease. He said that he intended to because he had assigned the rental payments to a local bank as collateral for a loan. The future rental payments were $5,200 per month for 30 months, or a little north of $150,000.

The appraiser told me that the cost of moving the equipment to the corporation's headquarters and leaving the plant "broom clean" for the next tenant would be around $20,000.

With these three numbers, I knew my offer would not exceed $250,000 in cash at closing, and I wanted the seller to guarantee the use of its approval codes for 6 months. This seems like a far cry from the $1,350,000 asking price. But it was realistic. The most that the corporation would be able to realize in liquidation was $226,000, viz:

Liquidation Value	$396,000
Less: Future Lease Payments, Moving, and Clean-Up Expenses	150,000 20,000
Total Deductions	170,000
Net Realizable Cash	$226,000

I also learned about a city guarantee that would back up an equipment loan. The guarantee was based on job creation or jobs saved, and 50 jobs were at stake. The city's formula for granting guarantees was $10,000 per job saved or created. I received a verbal yes that the plant would qualify for a loan guarantee. I visited several banks and called two equipment leasing companies. They said that subject to reviewing the city's guarantee, they would look favorably on advancing $300,000. They wanted to see $20,000 in equity invested.

The reason for the guarantee was because the plant had never made money and in the eyes of a lender that means it will never make money.

With $300,000 available, I needed an estimate of the amount of working capital I would need to kick-start the plant and pay for working capital and overhead expenses before the business reached break-even. This meant finding someone from the industry to run the plant postacquisition and lining up some orders from the plant's customers.

I called the plant's largest customers first. They told me that they needed product and would order product as soon as we were up and running. I said, "That won't work. I need your commitments now in order to save the plant from the auctioneer's hammer."

They replied, "If we give you our forward commitments now, what will you give us?"

"I'll give you exclusive markets," I replied.

And, in this manner, I closed three large customers that agreed to purchase, in the aggregate, $300,000 per month. I guaranteed that the plant would operate at above break-even and would employ at least 54 people. The city guarantee fell into place. The loan fell into place.

But the seller was intractable. It wanted a higher price. To solve this problem, I raised the back-end fee, and by showing the seller my operating statement projections, it bought the deal: $250,000 in the form of cash at closing and 10 percent of net profits before taxes for five years. I also agreed to the seller's form of press release in which they took credit for leaving the community only after they were assured that a new buyer was in place and jobs would be added rather than sacrificed.

14

HEALTH INSURANCE AND LITIGATION DEALS

Until recently, you and I would call upon the services of the professionals in the *distress* business—physicians and attorneys—and pretty much take them at their word and pay the bill they submitted when it was presented to us. That doesn't happen anymore, at least not nearly as much as it used to. Some of them are overbilling and overprescribing and, in the case of lawyers, overlitigating because unless they do so they will not be able to survive.

Doctors and lawyers are in business. We must deal with them. This means achieving clarity upfront, putting fee agreements in writing, and trying to achieve discounts and cash conserving arrangements with them just as if they were selling a used car. This unhappy circumstance has come about through a strict adherence to the Adam Smith Greed-Is-Good philosophy.

The nation's barometer of greed in business and in certain professions has achieved new heights. A growing list of executives and professionals have crossed the line from greed to unethical behavior and have been shot down, captured, and either imprisoned or persuaded to sing, or both.

THE GREED-IS-GOOD PHILOSOPHY

Economic philosophers have brought the commandments down to us from Mt. Adam Smith and proclaimed that they are truth and beauty. For instance, shortly after Ivan Boesky pleaded guilty in the fall of

1986, economist Irving Kristol saluted Adam Smith and aligned his moral philosophy with that of Hillel and the Talmud. When Hillel was asked to recite the entire body of ethical instruction while he stood on one foot, he responded with one sentence: "What is repugnant to you, do not do unto others; all the rest is commentary."[*] Adam Smith's principal contribution, says Kristol, is in proclaiming the market economy as a "good" place in the Talmudic sense of the word. Smith pointed out "how the sum of self-interested, economic actions, in themselves non-moral, resulted in an institution—the market economy—that was moral because it permitted everyone to better his condition even though each participant sought only his particular good."[**] Thus, the end justifies the means in the Smith/Kristol construction, notwithstanding Kristol's reference to the Talmud that states that repugnant means should be avoided.

The Smith/Kristol greed-is-good philosophy has accelerated a high-speed chase for short-term wealth. This breeds a cancer on the body economic known as *situational ethics*, or the justification of means because the ends are good: more wealth, family happiness, or the other side would have done it to me so I did it first (the inverse Golden Rule). Situational ethics is described in the following parable:

Two men are walking in the woods with heavy backpacks when they spot a very big, very angry grizzly bear. The bear roars at the men, who turn and run. One of the men sits down to take off his backpack.

"What are you doing that for?" asks the other fellow. "Don't you know you have to outrun the bear?"

To which he replies, "No, I don't. I just have to outrun you."

THE GREED-IS-NOT-GOOD PHILOSOPHERS

Kenneth J. Arrow and Frank N. Hahn argue that the Smith/Kristol thesis may have fueled the current high level of greed. Arrow and Hahn write: "Adam Smith...sought to show that a decentralized economy

---

[*]   Talmud, "Gemara Shabbat," p. 31.
[**] Irving Kristol, *The Wall Street Journal*, November 1986.

motivated by a self-interest and guided by price signals would be compatible with a coherent disposition of economic resources that could be regarded, in a well-defined sense, as superior to a large class of possible alternative dispositions.... It is important to understand how surprising this claim must be to anyone not exposed to the tradition. The immediate common sense answer to the question 'What will an economy motivated by individual greed and controlled by a very large number of different agents look like?' is probably: There will be chaos."[*]

HEALTH CARE DELIVERY

A growing number of physicians are prescribing unnecessary diagnostic procedures, upgrading diagnoses, and overprescribing pharmaceuticals to their patients in order to achieve larger reimbursements from health insurance carriers. This has pushed the nation's health care bill to nearly $500 billion per annum (it jumped nearly 10 percent in 1989 alone while inflation was 4.4 percent) and the money to pay the bill is no longer available. The physicians claim the tests are necessary to forestall litigation, and they are correct in part. But passing the buck by claiming another party *betrayed* you is as old an excuse as Adam's anger at Eve.

THE MARKETPLACE OF LAWYERS

The number of practicing lawyers in the United States increased from 265,823 in 1967 to over 700,000 in 1989—a 165 percent increase in 20 years. The market for lawyers is glutted. Yet, U.S. law schools continue to graduate 35,000 lawyers a year in the face of a severe decline in qualified applicants.

Lawyers vindicate Say's law that supply creates its own demand. When lawyers are climbing over one another to find work (note the

---

[*] Arrow, Kenneth J., and Frank N. Hahn, *General Competitive Analysis*, San Francisco, 1971.

prevalence of legal advertising), their response to the threat of un-
employment is to create work by encouraging people to sue one
another. "These low quality lawyers lack the ability to enter the
demanding fields like tax law and administrative law...and inevitably
turn their energies to ambulance chasing."[*] As a result, business
must pay for a military establishment to avoid being caught unawares
and abdicating their decision-making power to the courts.

Moreover, the rise in litigation is impacting the global compet-
itiveness of American manufacturers seriously, and the hidden tax
of product liability insurance can be felt in the nation's trade deficit.
Other countries, such as Japan, are not paralyzed in the vise of tort
liability. Their exports do not bear the hidden tax of legal fees and
insurance against tortuous claims that Peter W. Huber says costs
American consumers $300 billion per annum.[**] Our courts have swept
away the sanctity of contracts and ushered in LOTTO for lawyers.
"Something's gone wrong, let's work it out," the motto of rational
markets, has been replaced with "Something's gone wrong, whom
can we sue?"

HOW SPECULATORS CLOSE DEALS

Speculators normally move into markets when they detect a price
move in one direction or the other and correct the movement at a
profit to themselves. Speculators make deals with *price*. The miracle
of the marketplace is that in taking care of themselves, speculators
somehow ensure that producers all over the world will provide the
right quantity and quality of goods, without undue waste, and that
this meshes with what people want and the money they have available.

As economist and futures market speculator Victor Niederhoffer
writes:

> When a harvest is too small to satisfy consumption at its normal
> rate, speculators come in, hoping to profit from the scarcity by
> buying. Their purchases raise the price, thereby checking consumption

---

[*] Judge Richard Neely, *Judicial Jeopardy*, 1986.
[**] Peter W. Huber, *Liability*, Basic Books, Inc., New York, 1988.

so that the smaller supply will last longer. Producers encouraged by the high price further lessen the shortage by growing or importing to reduce the shortage. On the other side, when the price is higher than the speculators think the facts warrant, they sell. This reduces prices, encouraging consumption and exports and helping to reduce the surplus.
*

DEALS YOU CAN MAKE TO REDUCE HEALTH CARE

Greed is self-interest in a market of depletable resources. Adam Smith did not visualize the overgrazed commons that are certain American markets, such as health care and the legal profession, two hundred fifteen years after he brought forth his exegesis. He could not have forecast physicians or lawyers grabbing at a diminishing supply of patients and clients or flabby corporations. Quite simply, there is a shrinking supply of tired old bodies to heal and tired old products to hang tortuous claims on in a world of hungry physicians and lawyers. The result is runaway greed, situational ethics, intensive litigation, heavy firepower RICO, chaos, and eventually courtroom control of the boardroom.

To prevent our garden from being depleted by the Greed-Rico war, here are some deals you can make to reduce health care and litigation costs.

Utilization Review Companies

As the debate rages over who is responsible for the multiplication of drugs and diagnostic tests, *utilization review companies* are selling protection to beleaguered employers.

Utilization review companies are sleuths that use computers to track the procedures of physicians that are members of Preferred Provider Organizations (PPOs) or Health Maintenance Organizations (HMOs). When they spot a blip on their screens, such as more than half of the babies delivered by an Ob-Gyn within a certain period

---

* "The Speculator as Hero," *The Wall Street Journal*, February 10, 1989, p. A-8. Reprinted here with permission.

were by Caesarean section, they pay the doctor a visit to "remind" him or her to bring costs back in line. The PPO is the tollgate and its subsidiary, the Utilization Review (UR), is the "enforcer." Elliot A. Segal, president of National Capital Preferred Provider Organization in Washington, D.C., told *The Wall Street Journal* that the woodshed talk is "a way of putting somebody on notice in a subtle but telling way."

Doctor, Your Patient Will See You Now

Healthcare Compare Corporation, Lombard, Illinois, a publicly held utilization review company with 1989 revenues of $23 million and earnings of $1.8 million, has been monitoring physicians for five years on behalf of PPOs and insurance companies to eliminate unnecessary procedures. The UR helped Murray Industries, the Florida manufacturer of pleasure boats, reduce its health care costs 22 percent. Another client, Park 'n Fly Service, a parking lot operator in St. Louis, reported a reduction of 27 percent, without sacrificing quality of care.

Under UR, physicians use their traditional system of charging a fee for services rendered, but the procedures have to be approved by either Healthcare Compare or one of the other three hundred UR companies (or divisions of PPOs) currently in operation. A typical UR fee is $1.25 to $2 per employee per month. A UR has a staff of nurses and doctors, and in 60 percent of the cases the UR's nurses approve the procedures. The other diagnoses are reviewed by the UR's staff physicians. Emergency operations are done immediately, without consultation.

Because HMO physicians charge a fixed fee, the continued growth of URs, which bird-dog non-HMO physicians, for the most part augurs for the expansion of the PPO.

How Effective Is the PPO?

Lockheed-Georgia, a 20,000-employee subsidiary of Lockheed Corporation, joined the SouthCare Medical Alliance PPO in 1988 and slashed its employee costs by $500,000, according to Donald Meader, Coordinator of PPOs for Lockheed-Georgia. "We think that's only the beginning," Meader says. "We hope to do as well with dental, drugs, and therapy costs."

"The answer to delivering lower costs to employers via the PPO system," says Larry Madlem, who manages SouthCare, "is to deal with physicians as if they were travel agents and hospitals as if they were airlines. The smart physicians know they'll sell the most tickets if they deliver the lowest cost fares and offer prompt, efficient service. Once you have that understanding, the smart insurance companies—the ones without HMOs—will line up for your business."

The SouthCare Way

Larry Madlem learned the employee healthcare business at John Deere, Inc., the Moline, Illinois, farm equipment manufacturer that dived headfirst into health care cost containment in 1971. Deere has *its own insurance program* and reinsurance company, and its health care costs per employee were $110 per month in 1988. When Madlem felt that he understood the health care financing problem and how he might provide an effective solution, he left Deere and formed SouthCare. In addition to Lockheed-Georgia, Madlem has signed dozens of corporations and institutions representing 150,000 insured employees from Atlantic Steel Corporation, International Brotherhood of Electrical Workers, and the Glaziers Union.

For providers, SouthCare went after the lower-cost hospitals in Atlanta, primarily the not-for-profits, because they attract the lower-cost physicians. To qualify for membership in SouthCare, a provider must agree to bill at 15 to 20 percent less than the standard fee for a particular procedure. An employee can go outside the SouthCare network to select his or her own physician, but SouthCare will pay only 80 percent of the fee.

With the ability to deliver savings of 20 percent or more on healthcare costs to employers, SouthCare has attracted 26 insurance companies to underwrite the program. The insurance companies—CNA, Guardian, John Hancock, Massachusetts Mutual—put their logos on the program and sell it to SouthCare's members. The programs are essentially the same although the logos are different. Employees can select the carrier that appeals most to them.

You can see the power of the PPO and the UR in lowering your company's health care costs when you realize that the nation's 180 PPOs employ a total of twenty-four hundred people. Founded in 1985, SouthCare currently has nine hundred member physicians and eleven hospitals. It manages its tollgate with a mere eight employees.

ROLLING BACK LEGAL COSTS

Among U.S. corporations, legal expenses have become the second largest overhead item. It is essential for deal-makers to learn how to roll back legal expenses from 15 to 20 percent of net operating income to half that level.

A few years ago, I was sued in a California court for fraud, breach of contract, and mental anguish. It was a nuisance lawsuit without substance, but lawsuits must be responded to within thirty days or the defendant loses the suit. My local attorney failed to respond, and I lost by default. The default judgment awarded $3 million to the plaintiff.

No people are more keenly aware of the relative skills within their trade than are professional athletes and commercial litigators. Their box scores, wins, and losses are published daily. Therefore, when I called the best litigators I knew in New York and Chicago, plus those referred to me by business acquaintances with scar tissue from recent legal battles, I asked them to recommend the sharpest commercial litigators in the San Francisco Bay area.

Upon receiving the list, I boiled it down to three names, based on their immediate availability, hourly rates, and confidence levels. I interviewed these three firms until I found the lawyer who I felt was the most (credibly) hopeful, intelligent, and experienced and who, in addition, genuinely liked the case. His estimated fee was around $17,000, of which I agreed to pay half upfront, with the balance to be invoiced.

Within thirty days my lawyer turned the default judgment around and defeated the claim. I was, of course, relieved. He then asked me to send him a copy of the insurance policy my company maintains to pay for accidents should someone trip on a rug. Curious about his strategy, I sent him the policy and within two weeks he returned the $17,000 I had paid him, courtesy of the insurance company. When I asked him how come, he said, "In California, mental anguish is a personal injury and your insurance policy covered my expenses because the lawsuit included a claim for mental anguish."

Moral: *To reduce legal costs, review all of your company's insurance policies carefully to see how many risks are insured.* The process of insuring for essentially all business risks and having lawsuits and legal expenses paid by your insurers probably means that all litigious lawyers and clients will sue for every perceived injury until, eventually, there will be no insurance companies willing to indemnify any risk. But for now there exists, somewhere, an insurance company that will buy your company's risks, and in so doing lower your legal expenses dramatically.

Directors' and Officers' Insurance

The best money you can spend to throw an all-purpose shield around your company is D&O insurance. This policy indemnifies the company's officers and directors for errors and omissions in carrying out the objectives of the company. It does not protect the company in the event of fraud, misfeasance, malfeasance, or gross negligence, but for honest errors and mistakes D&O insurance is a necessary umbrella on a rainy day.

For example, suppose your controller makes a serious accounting error and fails to pay the company's withholding taxes for a year. The excuse: saving the company cash. But the IRS wants its $250,000 and is threatening to levy your company's bank accounts and other liquid assets.

A company without D&O insurance might call its lawyer, who, for a $25,000 legal fee, will negotiate a settlement. (Unpaid withholding taxes can always be settled, but never compromised—and are always stretched out. The IRS is comfortable with a six-month stretch, but I have heard of substantially longer installment plans.)

Depending on the terms of the D&O policy, the insurer may also pay approximately 90 percent of the unpaid withholding taxes.

Thus, for the cost of the policy, the withholding taxes will be paid by the D&O insurer *if* the nonpayment was not a fraudulent act. D&O insurance policies are more expensive per capita for small companies than they are for businesses of fifty or more employees. Policies cost between $6,000 and $12,000 per year, and you should ask your insurance agent to research the marketplace for you.

Acting as Your Own Counsel

To take another bite out of legal expenses, have your most meticulous employees draft some of the more routine contracts needed to operate your business. Scottie Williams, a creative inventor with over twenty patents to his name, publishes a handbook that he sells for $26. It explains how anyone can file a patent and protect an invention in the U.S. for less than $600. Most patent lawyers won't talk to a company for less than a $2,500 retainer. Williams's pamphlet dispels all the myths surrounding patents and takes the pain out of the process. For a copy of *Inventor's Workbook,* call Williams at 1-800-456-IDEA.

At the vanguard of the do-it-yourself law movement is Nolo Press, Berkeley, California, a publisher of self-help books for companies and individuals who seek to lower their legal fees. Nolo, which in Latin means "I do not choose to," has sixty titles in circulation. Over 200,000 readers have bellied up to Nolo's layperson's bar to buy its publications.

Legal Referees

Some lawyers occasionally cross the line between bold advocacy and breaches of ethics. Some overprescribe, misdiagnose, or underperform. When this happens, ask your state's bar association or disciplinary commission to intervene. Neither can grant monetary relief, but here is what they can do, in descending order of severity:*

---

* American Bar Association.

Disbarment: The lawyer may be disbarred and prohibited from practicing law in the state. Disbarment is usually imposed for criminal actions or gross misconduct bordering on crime.

Suspension: The lawyer may be suspended from practicing law for a period ranging from one day to several years, depending on the nature of the improper conduct.

Public Reprimand: The lawyer may be sanctioned by the highest court in the state and the sanction may be cited in the newspaper.

Private Reprimand: This is the lightest of wrist-slaps, intended only to establish a record for reference in the event of further misbehavior.

A word of warning, however: The law firms in the state pay fees to these two referees; fees that provide them with the wherewithal to hire staff and serve the public. Like most regulatory agencies, the referees of legal disputes follow Milton Friedman's law, which states that the regulatory agencies, to justify their existence, will support the industry they are empowered to regulate. Just remember—the layperson is *not* the client of the bar associations or disciplinary commissions.

More Cuts In Legal Costs

Most companies use their lawyers inefficiently. For example, when a firm sends a team of three lawyers to explain a legal problem, the company's employees fail to ask two of them to leave the room. The scope of the legal services required can usually be determined by one lawyer in less than thirty minutes. Also, most companies do not put their legal requirements out for bid and then interview many lawyers at different firms. Nor, when someone refers a lawyer to your company, do they ask why this lawyer, in particular, will help your company. For all you know, the person making the referral may be earning psychological or reciprocity points but may not be putting you into the best hands. Probe for the reasons.

Controlling the Billing

Discuss billing rates before the engagement. Discuss the way you wish to be billed—contingency, hourly rate paid monthly, or per event. Many lawyers prefer that you pay a retainer upfront (bankruptcy lawyers quite properly want 90 percent of their expected fee upfront) and then work the retainer off in hours. This is an appropriate arrangement for a complicated lawsuit or for a matter that has an uncertain ending, such as an acquisition or public offering. It is inappropriate for the drafting of a contract. Prepare a budget with your lawyer before the task begins, and monitor the budget.

Be sure to specify that you want fully itemized bills, ones that breakdown each hour or fraction thereof and describe how the time was spent. Question billed items that you don't understand. For example, your lawyer may not have to travel first class. If he or she does not work for you while traveling, he or she should not bill you for travel time.

Roy H. Park, the innovator of Duncan Hines Days and now the owner of broadcast properties and newspapers, recommends telephone calls rather than visits to lawyers. He keeps a "talk sheet" by the telephone, invites members of management into the room, and puts the lawyer on the speaker phone. When the conversation is over, the time is noted and the talk sheet is typed and filed in the legal costs folder, where it can be compared with the lawyer's monthly bill when it arrives.

When to Go In-House

If your company is consistently spending more than $75,000 a year on legal fees it is time to consider hiring in-house counsel. However, most in-house lawyers can't handle the "big case" or the specialized issues—environmental, tax, securities, antitrust—or litigation away from home.

If in-house counsel can be grafted on to other assignments such as corporate finance or fund-raising, you may get two tasks filled by the same person. Legal training is intensely analytical, and many lawyers are excellent acquisition analysts and financial planners. The

EDS division of General Motors recently announced a reduction in outside counsel from eighty-five to twelve firms.

Cooperating with Competitors

Find other companies to share your legal costs on matters that affect a region or an industry, such as handling industrial wastes, environmental clean-ups, and massive tort litigation for inadequate labeling or product safety features. The formation of coalitions is gaining popularity in administrative agency proceedings and local zoning matters.

Join with your competitors: Agree not to retain a law firm whose litigation department sues any company in your industry on a product liability matter. But first, *ask* the government if this is a violation of antitrust laws.

Using Arbitration Instead of Court Litigation

The American Arbitration Association handles 40,000 cases each year. It draws on the services of 60,000 arbitrators, many of whom are experts in a particular business or industry. An arbitrator has the authority to enter a binding, court-enforceable judgment from which only the most limited kind of appeal will be allowed. The fee for arbitrating a $10,000 case is $300.

When your company enters into a contractual arrangement with another company, make certain that a future dispute will be resolved by arbitration. The following language in the contract is recommended:

> In the event of any dispute between you and (Company), you and (Company) agree to resolve them through the auspices of the American Arbitration Association in (City, State). Any award rendered shall be final and conclusive upon the parties. The prevailing party shall be entitled to his or her costs and reasonable attorneys' fees in connection with such arbitration and the enforcement thereof.

Rent-a-Judge

An alternative to arbitration would be to hire the services of a retired judge to handle disputes. Several entrepreneurial companies are now hiring retired judges who decide cases much more rapidly than does the nation's overloaded legal system. In addition, legal fees are reduced because cases brought in private courts do not require as much documentation or as many procedural mechanisms. Both parties must agree in writing to resolve their dispute either in this way or by arbitration and that neither will appeal the decision to state or federal court.

The Price of Impulsivity

Legal fees can get away from you if you aren't vigilant. Especially in matters such as a drop-everything-this-is-an-emergency lawsuit or a large financing. Before calling the company's lawyer in panic—"I don't care if he is in a conference, Estelle, this is an emergency"— remember this: You'll pay for impulsiveness. Lawyers have twenty-five hundred billable hours to sell each year, and my experience has been that lawyers are compulsive invoicers and that they adore impulsive clients.

The impulsive use of lawyers will add 30 percent to your legal bills. Before you call your lawyer, stop. Ask yourself: Is the private placement far enough along? Is the acquisition real? Are the terms agreed to? Can we handle the matter in-house at this stage? What will it cost the company in legal fees if it aborts?

The price of being impulsive, of thinking that each of your CEO's most creative ideas requires a lawyer to sanctify them from the start, will cost the company big-time dollars. There is a time, a place, and a way to use legal services; and knowing when and how to use them can save bundles of cash.

CHAPTER 15

JAPANESE DEALS

The Japanese have been providing over $100 billion per annum in fresh capital to the U.S. economy for the last decade. Some politicians raise their well-oiled voices in a cacophony of shock and dismay about our sell-out to the Japanese, but they are misguided. We need fresh capital at the domestic poker table and the Japanese are long-term players. "Their horizons are incredibly long," a securities analyst who follows the Japanese stock market told me. "In America, five years is the long-term. In Japan, one hundred years is the long-term."

DOES YOUR DEAL FIT THE NEEDS OF JAPANESE CONSUMERS?

The process of closing Japanese investors begins with research to determine if your deal fits their criteria. The Japanese are a highly literate culture. They publish hundreds of magazines and newsletters and the pages are full of pictures of American products and articles about new products and services budding in American shops and offices.

Japanese magazine readers are fearful of *dasai*—being out of it and behind the times—so they flock to trend-information magazines. The most popular have American names: *Popeye* for college-aged young men; *Brutus*, for men in their 20s; *Olive* for teenage girls;

and *Tarzan*, for the sports conscious. "The Japanese tend not to be put off by being told what they should do," says Suetomo Takaoka, a media buyer at Dentsu, Inc., Japan's biggest ad agency. Rather, he says, "they feel grateful," for updates on trends they think everybody else probably already knows about.*

Nikkei, the Japanese equivalent of *The Wall Street Journal*, sends reporters to America continually to discover what is new. I recently spent an afternoon with a Nikkei reporter, and he enumerated his interests as the following:

- Consumer products that can be sold through vending machines. (Japan is the most heavily-vended country on the planet.)

- Direct mail marketing services. (This form of marketing is relatively unknown in Japan.)

- Franchises that can be exported to Japan. (When Kentucky Fried Chicken opened a store in Japan, lines formed around the block.)

ECONOMIC GAMES THE JAPANESE PLAY

Pioneers get arrows in their backs. Honed on Western movies, or perhaps it is their indigenous culture, the Japanese do not leap into a market first. They follow. Americans play a game known as *Quick Draw*. The Japanese play *After You, Garçon* and *Cooperative Quick Draw*. Let's see how these games work.

Quick Draw

Company executives reason: If I go ahead and innovate while my competitors play it safe, I stand to make big profits. If I play it safe while they take the plunge, I save R&D spending but lose out on big profits. If we all play it safe, things stay as they are. If we all take the plunge, the market may be too small for all of us and there may be big losses, at least initially.

---

* Yumiko Ono, "Magazine House: Tokyo's Trend-Setter," *The Wall Street Journal*, June 27, 1991, p. B–1.

What the company does depends critically on what it perceives its competitors will do. If the expectation is that competitors will take the plunge, the best bet for the company is to play it safe and avoid big losses. If the company thinks its competitors will play it safe, the right move is to take the plunge, to thus earn big profits. As in the Old West, you draw on your opponent when you think you are faster. When both gunfighters err and draw simultaneously, they wind up in Boot Hill. For example, in the early days of mainframe computers, several large corporations, including RCA and General Electric, "drew" simultaneously—and ended up burying their computer divisions under heavy losses.

Minnetonka, Goliath, and Softsoap

A real-world example of *Quick Draw* is the saga of Minnetonka, Goliath and Softsoap. In 1980, a small Minnesota-based company named Minnetonka, Inc., introduced a new product, Softsoap—liquid soap dispensed from a squirt gun by a touch of the finger. Consumers liked it. They found it was clean, did not mess up soap dishes, did not shrink to infuriating slivers, and you didn't slip on it in the shower or bathtub.

While Goliath—giant rivals like Procter & Gamble, Armour-Dial, Lever Bros., and Colgate-Palmolive—played safe, Minnetonka sold $35 million worth of Softsoap in the first year. It then chose to plunge ahead and spend close to that amount ($30 million) on advertising and promotion alone in 1981—half of it devoted to distributing 200 million coupons. Minnetonka general manager Wallace Marx said, "This is high-stakes poker. It's going to cost a lot to get in and a lot to stay in." A competing company's executive commented early in 1981, "You can never be sure about trying to change consumer habits. I'm not ready to jump on the bandwagon yet."*

In *Quick Draw*, the price of error is very high. Large corporations may be run by executives less eager to make big profits (at big

---

* Shlomo and Sharone L. Matial, *Economic Games People Play*, Basic Books, Inc., New York, 1984, pp. 86–89.

risk) than to avoid large losses. The Japanese do not play *Quick Draw*, but rather *After You, Garçon*.

In contrast to *Quick Draw*, big profits are seen to accrue not to the first to "take the plunge" but to the third or fourth player. Alacrity implies making costly errors and incurring big expenses from which other firms can benefit. If the company thinks its competitors will take the plunge, its best strategy is to play it safe and wait.

In *After You, Garçon*, there is again no dominant, best-in-every-case strategy. A cautious innovator who wants to minimize losses will play it safe. The worst he or she can do then is break even. When all game players reason that way, everyone plays it safe. The Japanese buyer reasons that the best time to deal with procrastination is tomorrow, and they make their moves accordingly.

Japanese reasoning is, let someone else pioneer new technologies, change consumer preferences, develop new markets, and risk his or her neck. Once he or she has broken untilled soil, we can farm it at our ease.

HOW TO CONTACT JAPANESE BUYERS

As in all deals, you want to make your contact as close to the top of the power oligarchy as possible. If it takes a finder to get you there, so much the better. Visit a large public library and review a directory called Martindale Hubbell. It lists law firms and their clients. The New York, San Francisco, and Los Angeles firms represent the largest number of Japanese companies. There are other directories of finders, including *The Middle Market Business Acquisition Directory and Source Book*, A. David Silver, Harper Collins, New York, and *The Directory of Deal-Makers*, Tweed Publishing Company, Tiboron, California. Both directories list plenty of finders with Japanese contacts.

You can also go to the Japanese companies directly. Many of them have New York, Los Angeles, or San Francisco offices. The white pages of big-city telephone books can provide you with the telephone numbers, and from there, ask for the Chief Executive Officer's secretary.

Presenting the Deal

Japanese buyers cannot say "no." So they don't say "yes." (And there is no word for "maybe.") As long as you avoid the "no," you still have a shot at the "yes."

To avoid the "no" and to get the "yes," make sure to present a summary of the deal: no more than two pages. A complete plan with exhibits will simply not be read because the very act of reading it suggests a "yes."

If the summary is reviewed and well-received, you will then have the opportunity to present the full deal; first orally, and then in written form. Here's the catch, however: If at any time, by oversight or a sudden alteration in the deal, you say something that is different, even if immaterial, from what is printed in the deal memorandum, you will have lost the trust of the Japanese buyers and your deal will die. It will not be turned down. You will merely never get a second audience.

It goes without saying that trend-following deals are of greater interest to the Japanese than are trend-setting. Japanese buyers are not pioneers.

FUNDING THE DEAL: TWO STAGES

The Japanese tend to fund their American deals in two stages. The first stage involves a sum of money that the Japanese buyer can afford to lose. If he or she is pleased with how you spend the money, you will receive the second traunch. If not, you will not see the second stage money.

In 1990, Dai-Ichi Mutual Life Insurance Company agreed to buy the Preferred Stock of Lincoln National Corporation, the holding company of several insurance companies, with assets of $29 billion. The preferred stock is convertible into 9.9 percent of Lincoln National's common stock. Dai-Ichi invested $150 million in 1990 and a second $150 million in 1991. The deal has been referred to as a "white knight" deal on Wall Street; that is, it warns possible raiders that Lincoln National will fight a possible takeover by jumping into the arms of Dai-Ichi. White knight deals act like a ceiling on the company's stock price because they block takeover attempts. On the other hand, senior managers get to keep their jobs.

Gift Giving

The Japanese buyer is an altruist. That is, he or she regards attention to a deal and eventual investment as a gift to you. In reciprocity, it is important that you give gifts to the Japanese buyer. Appropriate gifts at the first meeting are $25 to $75 souvenirs, photography or art books, or products related to what you are about.

A second gift is to offer to spend your own money to fly to Japan to meet the top executives who will make the ultimate decision to invest in your deal. This offer to fly to Japan typically results in their offer to visit you, but at least you made the gift-giving gesture.

"Why Not?"

Between the "yes" and the closing is the "why not?" The Japanese buyer will assign six or eight analysts to read your deal memorandum. They will read it many times looking for errors of fact or misstatements. If you say one thing, but print another, your deal is dead. But if everything is accurate in word, print, and deed, all the reasons for turning the deal down will have been brushed aside and the leader will ask his or her analysts, " Why not put in some money and see how it does?"

If nobody objects, you will receive the first investment: the "why not" investment. If you stick to the plan, the second investment will soon follow.

16

SMALL-MONEY DEALS THAT CAN ADD UP

Two deals a day keep the doctor away. The doctor in this case is "Doctor Deficits." I recommend a daily exercise regimen consisting of doing two small money-saving or money-making deals every day. They do not have to be large deals. Small ones, if done with regularity soon add up to money. First we will review money-savings deals, then cash-raising deals.

MONEY-SAVING DEALS

Your Landlord Is Overcharging You

Pull a copy of your lease out of the file, bring in your Stanley tape measure from home, and read these words carefully if you want to cut your company's office, plant, and warehouse rental expenses. You are probably paying for "rentable" space when you should be paying for "usable" space. The difference between the two is common areas in the building. Common areas include tenant's pro-rata share of the lobbies, corridors, restrooms, janitorial and electrical closets, vending and other areas that are shared by all tenants. If you are on an upper floor, your pro-rata usage of the lobby is less than that of a first floor tenant. Thus, your firm should pay less for the common area. Is it paying less for the lobby? Read the lease.

Common Area Factor

This is the square footage differential between rentable area and usable area. Rentable area includes the entire finished interior of a building's floor, including common areas such as restrooms, the lobby space, corridors, electrical closets, and janitorial closets. Usable area is the entire interior square footage of office space available for the private use of the tenant. The Building Owners and Managers Association (BOMA) has established standards for measuring usable space. These standards state the usable space should be calculated by measuring from the inside surface of the dominant portion of the permanent outer building walls to the office side of the corridor or other permanent walls, to the center of partitions that separate the office from other usable areas.

Landlords typically calculate a pro-rata share of the common area for each tenant and add that amount of space to usable area in order to create a number for rentable area. Then they base the rent on the larger number. The landlord's *loss factor*, which properly should be called *excess profit factor*, arises from charging for common area factors that the tenants simply never use. These include the janitor's closet and the air conditioning equipment room among others.

Internal Space Measurement

The second problem is that the measurement of the space your company is occupying for its office, plant, or warehouse is probably inaccurate. The landlord more than likely took the measurements from a blueprint or from the outer walls. Remeasure the space from the inner walls; carefully go around the buttresses with your tape measure; exclude the electrical and telephone boxes. Then compare your total square footage number with the number in the lease. I will bet that your number is the smaller one. Here are two examples of what you are likely to find:

Company ABC leases 5,780 sq. ft. of office space at $19.00 per square foot. An in-house measurement indicates a discrepancy of 578 sq. ft. or approximately 10 percent. Over a lease term of five years, the total recovery and/or savings could be $54,910. If taxes and ancillary services such as janitorial, security, insurance, utilities, and parking are taken into account, the overcharge claim would increase. If this company has 20 employees, that's a savings of over $2,500 per employee.

Company XYZ leases 30,500 sq. ft. of warehouse space at $9.50 per square foot. An in-house measurement indicates a discrepancy of 3,050 sq. ft. Over a lease term of ten years, the total recovery and/or savings would amount to $137,250, and more with the ancillary services.

Renegotiating Your Lease

Once you have discovered that you have been overcharged by your landlord, you probably have two amounts: an amount for miscalculating the usable area occupied by your office; and an amount for overcharging your company for the common area. BOMA has standards for helping you roll back the first amount while the second amount will require negotiation and cooperation with the other tenants. If there are no other tenants, you will have to renegotiate the lease with the landlord on your own.

If the landlord will not budge on refunding you for lease overcharges on either or both of your points—inaccurate usable space measurement or common factor overcharge—it is time for you to "sell protection." Although *The Godfather* is the business manual for learning this skill, earlier chapters that deal with *cooperation* and *tollgates* make the same points.

You leave the landlord's office and establish a tenant's cooperative. Lend your Stanley tape measure to the other tenants and ask them to do their calculations and meet with you. At the meeting, gather the data of usable space overcharges and common factor overcharges and prepare a memorandum for your cooperative to the landlord, requesting a meeting with all tenant association members to discuss the possibility of measurement errors. Tell your fellow tenants that because you are acting as the lightning rod, you are entitled to have your lease renegotiated first. Put this understanding in writing and have the other cooperative tenants sign it to avoid misunderstandings and possible litigation.

Make it very clear to the landlord that there is a tollgate to pass through before meeting with the tenants; that is, you operate a tollgate and before turning the pike the landlord will first have to deal with your lease situation. If you are satisfied with the results, you will be pleased to help in the renegotiations with other members of the association.

Reducing Postage Costs

If your business uses direct mail as a common advertising medium, wasted postage costs can add up to several hundred thousand dollars per year. Here are some tips to save postage costs.

Presorting Services

Major mailers, such as credit card companies and mail order houses, sort their mail by Zip Code before taking it down to the post office. The U.S. Postal Service offers them a 25 percent discount, or 5 cents off of a 29 cent mailing. The American Postal Workers Union, a 350,000 member union, argues that they could do the job just as well and they would like to see 2.5 cents of the discount in their paychecks. However, an independent government commission that reviews postal rates says that the presorting discount is a bargain.

But what about companies that generate 500 pieces of mail per day or less. If that is your situation, you can call on one of 250 privately-owned presorters located throughout the country. Presorters save you most of the 5 cents, which can add up to several thousand dollars per year, depending on volume.

Elodia Swenson, owner of American Presort, Inc., Brea, California, quit her job in 1987, rented a 1,700 sq. ft. space in an industrial park, lined the walls with wooden cubbyholes, and hired local high school students to sort the mail. She began calling on 500 companies in Orange County in her van, often bypassing the mailing department and speaking directly with the controller.

Customers came slowly while American Presort gained credibility. Today, with TRW, Inc., Knotts Berry Farm, and others as her customers, Ms. Swenson is presorting around 50,000 pieces of mail a day, which she told *The Wall Street Journal* is a breakeven level of operations.

Carrier Route Sorting

If your company is in the field of direct mail marketing or if it sends out thousands of third class envelopes each month, then your postage costs are $167 per 1,000 pieces, or 16.7 cents per envelope. This assumes that you are presorting by Zip Code. You can lower the cost to $101 per 1,000 pieces, or 10.1 cents per envelope, a savings of 33 percent, if you sort the envelopes by carrier routes.

Regional post offices will provide you with the names of their couriers and the addresses they cover if you ask them. You can obtain census maps from the U.S. Commerce Department and enlarge them. Then hire high school students to sort the envelopes by carrier routes. They will bundle them with rubber bands and write the name of the courier on the top of the bundle. Then take the bundles to the post offices.

When you use carrier route sorting you can be more assured that the mailing piece will be delivered in a timely manner.

Saving on Overnight Courier Expenses

Major corporations pay considerably less than do small and medium-sized companies to send an overnight package. The average cost to an ordinary user to send a one-pound package overnight is $14.50. Federal Express Corporation charges $20.25 for the same package, but it guarantees delivery by 10:30 A.M. the following morning. IBM Corporation and other large corporations are offered discounts by the overnight courier companies of up to 40 percent.

Jealous? You don't have to be if you *just ask* your courier for a discount. My firm ships from three to six packages per day, most of them one pound or less. We asked our courier for a discount, and here's what we received:

Figure 16.1
RATE COMPARISON FOR OVERNIGHT AIR COURIER
SERVICE WITH AND WITHOUT DISCOUNT

Weight (Lbs.)	With Standard Discount	Federal Express	DHL Express
Letter	$ 8.50	$ 14.00	$ 14.00
Pack	14.00	20.25	25.00
1 lb.	14.00	20.25	25.00
2 lbs.	15.00	23.00	25.00
3 lbs.	18.00	25.75	28.00
4 lbs.	21.00	28.50	31.00
5 lbs.	23.00	31.25	34.00
50 lbs.	68.00	95.00	89.00
90 lbs.	103.00	145.00	129.00

What does this mean to your company? Let's say your company
ships 400 packages per year, or about one every other day, and that
the average weight is two pounds. If you do not ask for a deal,
you will pay $9,200 per annum. But if you obtain a discount, you
will pay $6,000, a savings of $3,200 per annum. The real savings
occur with higher volume and big packages.

Telephone

Your company can purchase (or lease) interconnect telephone systems
that have a feature known as *least cost* routing. This feature relies
on a micro chip that automatically selects the least costly carrier
for a particular long distance call—WATS, AT&T, ALC, MCI, Sprint,
or Telenet. If you are in the service business and your telephone
calls are billed to a client or customer—law firm, hotel, hospital—you
can select an interconnect system with *call accounting/cost accounting*
that assigns each call to a specific telephone. "There is nothing that

so rapidly modifies the telephone behavior of employees than announcing that a call accounting system has been installed," says Donn Thielman, President of Aztec Communications, Inc., Palm Springs, California, a consulting firm that services the telecommunications needs of large corporations. "When we installed call accounting at Hughes, Texaco and Lockheed, their monthly telephone bills dropped 30 percent," says Thielman.

Code Toll Restriction

Interconnect systems also offer the ability to block certain telephones from calling certain area codes. This restriction blocks certain calls, let's say the accounts receivable department that calls the West Coast, from making calls to the other regions of the country to check in with Aunt Tillie and Uncle Mel. "Codes toll restriction will slash another 5 percent off the monthly telephone bill," reports Thielman.

Repackagers

The overnight courier repacking strategy has been applied to telephone costs as well. There are 12 telephone line repackagers in the country that buy hundreds of trunk lines at a reduced price each month from the major long distance carriers, which the carriers sell for 11 cents per minute. The repackagers pay a price of 5 cents per minute, and resell them for 8 cents per minute. Why not call on the repackager in your Yellow Pages and make a deal to lower your telephone charges?

Savings on Car Rentals

As a frequent traveler, I have become aware of certain anomalies in the car rental market that my travel agent does not know about. For instance, the Budget Car Rental yard is much closer to O'Hare Airport than are the others, perhaps 10 minutes closer. Budget is usually $2 to $15 cheaper per day than the other airport-based car rental companies are (unless they are running specials), and the time savings make them a first choice at O'Hare. At Los Angeles International Airport, Atlanta, LaGuardia, San Francisco, and other major metropolitan airports, the airport-based car rental companies have practically no time advantage over the nonairport-based ones because the car yards for all the companies are a mile or so from the airport. It will take you about 20 minutes to get behind the wheel of a rental car no matter which company you use, so you might as well use one of the off-airport car rental companies.

Following in Figure 16.2 are the comparative prices for a one-day rental of a mid-size car at a major airport:

Figure 16.2
COMPARABLE CAR RENTAL PRICES WITH TRANSPORT TIME FROM AIRPORT TO CAR YARD ASSUMED CONSTANT

Company	Telephone No.	One Weekday Rental Price
On-Airport		
Hertz	800-654-3131	$79.99 (70 free miles)
National	800-328-4567	64.95 (70 free miles)
Budget	800-527-0700	62.99 (70 free miles)(a)
Avis	800-331-1212	49.00 (no free miles)
Dollar	800-421-6868	39.95 (unlimited free miles)
Off-Airport		
Alamo	800-327-9633	43.99 (unlimited free miles)
Thrifty	800-367-2277	43.00 (150 free miles)
General	800-327-7607	39.95 (unlimited free miles)

(a)   or $72.99 with unlimited free miles.

Let's assume that your company's travelers fly into major airports, rent their cars for one day, and travel 100 miles. Further, assume that you have contacted the car rental companies and asked for their standard 15 percent discount. The travelers must be transported in a van to their cars, thus transport time is assumed to be constant. The savings on 100 trips per year by using an off-airport company is as follows:

	Average 1–Day Car Rental Price	Average Mileage at $.10/mi.	Less Discount	1–Day Costs	100–Day Costs
On-Airport	$64.25	$4.75	$(9.64)	$59.36	$5,936.00
Off-Airport	41.25	—	(6.20)	35.05	3,505.00
Difference	$23.00	$4.75	$(3.44)	$24.31	$2,431.00

Trapping for Gold in the Incoming Mail

One of the most significant benefits that deal-makers bring to their companies is the introduction of performance-based pay. When employees own stock or when they are entitled to a significant bonus tied to cash flow, they are kept better informed about the company's progress, and they can relate their performance on a one-to-one basis with the weight of their pay envelopes. This leads to a broadening ripple of employee-initiated money-saving deals.

I recently visited a company in which I saw the secretaries storing incoming third-class mail and catalogs behind their desks. I visited the lunchroom and saw that aluminum cans were being captured and saved. Here's what the secretaries told me: "We're cost centers, you know. But we get a bonus if we can cut our costs 10 percent by recycling trash."

The secretaries combine the incoming paper trash, such as magazines, catalogs, and third-class mail, with the not-quite-outgoing mail—first drafts, bad photostats, mistakes—and shop for the best recycling price they can find on this category of paper known as "mixed paper."

There are certain rules of the road to maximize your trash. Most paper recyclers will put several Gaylord boxes on pallets outside your back door at no charge. A Gaylord is a 4 foot by 4 foot by 4 foot box and holds 600 to 800 pounds of paper. Four full Gaylords make a ton. The paper recyclers like to see you sort the computer printer paper from the other trash because it is the most valuable.

The range of value for your paper trash is approximately as follows (these prices vary between metropolitan areas and with economic conditions):

Computer printer paper	$150/ton
Photostat paper	90/ton
Colored paper (catalogs)	20/ton
Newspapers	10/ton
Corrugated boxes	5/ton

After you presort the paper trash into categories, make certain you keep it dry. Put covers on the Gaylords or bring them inside if it looks like rain. Once paper becomes wet it loses its value.

Uses of Recycled Paper

Computer printer paper is recycled into the highest quality stationery. Photostat paper is recycled as medium grade bond. Mixed paper, your incoming mail, is recycled as inexpensive paper. And, in some markets, corrugated paper boxes and newspapers have a second life as cardboard and napkins. The recyclers in Miami, Florida, are no longer picking up newspapers because there is an excess of it.

How Much Can You Make?

Depending on the size of your company and its paper consumption, as well as its incoming mail, you might be able to fill your four to eight Gaylords 20 times a year and generate $3,400 to $6,800 annually. That's about the volume that several computer-literate firms of 100 to 200 employees told me they're generating each year.

Double Sided Photostating

One of the largest savings in paper costs can be generated by photostating reports on the front and back of each piece of paper. At $15 per pound of photostat paper, by using both sides your company might save $1,000 per year or more.

Cut FAX Cover Sheets In Half

Most FAX messages are sent with a cover sheet that has your company's logo on it, the name of the receiver, its FAX number, the date of the message, the time of the message, the sender's name and number, and the total number of pages being FAXed. This entire gaggle of information can be put on one-half of an 8-1/2 inch by 11 inch piece of paper.

There is a triple savings here. You will save 50 percent on cover sheets, 50 percent on storage space for used cover sheets (to be reconciled against the monthly telephone bills), and 50 percent on FAX charges. Assuming that one full page costs 17 cents to send in the U.S. and that your company sends 5,000 FAX messages per annum per machine, each with its own cover sheet, by going to half sheets the savings is $425 per year. Double that number for the value of the other two savings—paper and storage. If your company has 10 FAX machines, the savings could be over $8,000 per annum.

Employee Leasing

When is the last time somebody came up to you and made you this deal: I will take all of your employees on your payroll and rent them back to you. They will receive substantially improved health benefits and if you ever want to terminate any of them, I will find them another job. You can save the payroll costs of your human resources department—$20,000 per person at least. I will fill out all of the government and insurance forms for the employees, handle all terminations, and you will gain back extra time for other management tasks.

Tempting offer, isn't it? You can save money, avoid compliance hassles, and gain legions of time for important issues. On the other hand, you can remain in the more traditional groove of hiring people, firing people, negotiating benefits, and complying with an increasingly complex alphabet soup of government regulations. Managing employees reminds me of a sign I once saw on an old dirt road in South Georgia: "Pick your rut carefully 'cause you're going to be in it for the next 40 miles."

Faced with increasingly complex employee issues, you can make a deal to slash employee-related costs. Employee-leasing companies provide the following services that your company may rent.

- Process payroll checks.
- Provide you with weekly payroll and billing reports.
- File and pay all state and federal employer taxes.
- Prepare W-2 forms at year-end for all employees.
- Provide a comprehensive employee health insurance program.
- Process Section 125 benefits deductions.
- Process all insurance claims.
- Offer and administer COBRA benefits.
- Provide coverage for worker's compensation; issue certificates and administer claims.
- Administer state employment claims.
- Provide a credit union.
- Provide an in-house human resources consultant.
- Provide in-house legal counsel.

The average size company that leases its employees has a payroll of thirty people, and many of them are rapidly expanding companies whose managers are too busy steering their companies' growth to pay necessary attention to the obfuscated tautology of government and insurance compliance forms.

Walt Dixon, President of Wal-Tech, a yarn-dyeing facility for woven fabrics with 250 workers in three plants in three states, compared employee leasing with the services of a payroll firm and chose employee leasing. He told the Triangle *Business* newsweekly, "The amount of time I save on office work is immense. I spent 25 years dealing with people and payroll and all that goes with it, and I recognize the value of a package like this that will leave me not having to deal with life insurance agents, tax people, or anybody like that."

Summary

For the 100- to 300-employee company, deals you can make by employee leasing and negotiating a lease reduction with your landlord are worth $50,000 to $120,000 per year in free cash flow.

When you add in the savings in postage, overnight couriers, FAX, telephone, car rentals, and trash, the cost savings are substantial; and they show up in cash flow.

There are lots of cost-saving deals you can make if you keep your head under the hood and look. Now, let's look at small, more exciting deals that you can do every day to increase cash flow.

CASH-RAISING DEALS

Tips for Boosting Your Cash Flow

If your sales have declined because of the recession, try these steps to help you increase your cash flow substantially in less than sixty days:

1. *Capture Data on Customers:* Put a large fish bowl in the store near the cash register, and place a sign near it saying a drawing will occur in 30 days, with the winner to receive a special prize. Have customers fill out forms asking their name (to capture gender), birth date (to capture age), and address (to capture location). You'll find out who your customers are. Enter your customers' names and other information in a database and update weekly.

2. *Market Research:* Study the list. Are most of your customers women over 40? Or teenagers and children? Do they come from one ZIP Code or several? Do they drive or walk to your business? When you know the demographics of those who do shop at your store, you can target your marketing efforts more effectively to reach those who don't.

3. *Inexpensive Marketing Strategies:* Send birthday cards to customers, and offer them a 10 percent discount if they come

in with the card. Mail your customers a monthly newsletter/catalog, announcing specials, new products and services, and events at the store. In planning events, you could invite local apparel stores to have fashion shows in your establishment—particularly if it's a large restaurant. Invite local artists to hang their works on your walls, and charge them a sales commission.

4. *Public Relations:* Kill your advertising budget for a month by concentrating on "free advertising"; that is, public relations. You'll need something to talk about for the newspapers to pick up your story.

Here's a proven idea: "Buy a product; plant a tree." Give away a small pine seedling in a bag for any purchase of $20 or more. You can buy the seedlings from a local nursery or from Central Florida Lands & Timber Co., Perry, Florida, for $1.25 each. Then call the Boy Scouts, the Girl Scouts, schools, churches, and any associations involving children, and invite them to "buy a product; plant a tree." If 20 Scouts get 20 trees from you and plant them in a local park, the newspapers will say where they got them—your store—and many more customers will come in to buy from you. And if 20 Scouts buy or receive 20 trees, they or others will have paid you $400 for products. And you will have captured their names and their parents' names for your customer mailing list.

5. *Air Space Marketing:* Put racks and buckets at the ends of aisles and carry high-markup items in these spaces, which previously were not retail spaces; hence, the phrase "air space." Greeting cards, refrigerator magnets, potpourri, key chains, and similar items usually carry sufficiently high margins for this.

6. *Find Noncustomers:* Enter into joint-ventures with local large department stores with whom you are not in competition—to put your mailer into their monthly invoices. It will be sent to hundreds of thousands of their customers, not yours. If a recipient comes into your store carrying one of these "stuffers," you can give that person a 10 percent discount, and you can pay the department store 20 percent of the retail selling price for the cost of using its monthly billing envelope.

7. *Come Fly With Me:* Copy the airlines. Offer a "Frequent Shopper Club" discount. In your newsletter, announce a series of prizes for customers who spend $100 a month at your store, $250 a month, or $500 a month. The prizes can be discounts or free trips. You can tie in the program with Visa or MasterCard for an added plus, and the card companies might rent you their lists in your best ZIP Codes.

8. *Back-Door Marketing:* As your list of customers grows, you can begin to rent it to large magazine publishers and credit card firms at the rate of 7 cents per name. Let's say you capture 5,000 names and rent the list to 20 direct-marketing firms. That's 100,000 name rentals at 7 cents apiece, or $7,000.

Note that in all these suggestions, you wouldn't have to spend much money to increase traffic—perhaps $5,000 for computer services and for preparing a small coupon to be stuffed into the department stores' monthly billing envelopes. But you would reap benefits, such as cutting your advertising expenses to the bone, generating two or three times more traffic, and, best of all, capturing noncustomers and converting them to customers.

We have covered a lot of ground together, and I'll bet you're feeling like you've been rode hard and hung up wet, as Gabby Hayes used to tell Roy Rogers. You may find yourself in deals where you need someone to talk with, someone to kick around closing strategies with. I will be pleased if that someone is me. You can contact me by writing to me in care of the publisher. I can't guarantee results: Remember what I said about personal guarantees. But I will promise to give it my best shot.

Index